LIFE ASCENDING

UNLOCKING MENTAL WELLBEING THROUGH TIMELESS WISDOM AND NEW SCIENCE

DAVID W YOUNGREN

Anora
PRESS

CONTENTS

INTRODUCTION

We live in a world full of diversity, rich with endless possibilities and unique experiences. From the rustling of leaves in the wind to the vibrant hues of a sunset, from the sound of a loved one's laughter to the comforting aroma of a favorite meal, our senses open a window to the world around us. Yet, while we share the same physical space, our perceptions of life and reality can be vastly different.

These differences come from our deeply held beliefs—whether they stem from religion, politics, culture, or personal values—and from the emotional highs and lows we experience. Our beliefs shape how we see the world, while our experiences, both joyful and painful, leave lasting marks that influence how we react to what life throws at us.

We might witness the same event, hear the same words, or even share the same moment with others but interpret it in entirely different ways. Our past experiences and beliefs color our perspective. A movie that makes one person laugh might move another to tears. A speech that inspires one person might offend someone else. The same event could bring joy to some and sadness to others.

At our core, we all long for love, happiness, and a meaningful life. We seek connection, to be understood, and to make our own mark on the world. But our differing perceptions and experiences often create barriers to these desires. Misunderstandings arise, conflicts flare up, and dissatisfaction lingers when our personal realities collide with those of others.

On top of this, we wrestle with our own inner struggles—anxiety, guilt, self-doubt—that warp how we see ourselves and the world. These internal battles can make it even harder to connect with others, understand our circumstances, and find the fulfillment we seek, adding yet another layer to the complexity of being human.

But imagine living with a perception grounded in inner peace, unconditional love, and deep wisdom. Envision how this shift would transform your everyday life—strengthening your relationships, enhancing your mental wellbeing, and filling you with a renewed sense of purpose. Such a change in awareness not only has the potential to elevate our lives but to positively impact entire communities and humanity as a whole. This is the essence of the ascending life—a state of being where peace and love unlock the gateway to a limitless reality, abundant with wisdom, creativity, and purpose.

"It's Not Working for Me...."

For many, the idea of an idyllic, ascending life may seem like nothing more than a fantasy. Despite their best efforts —through religion, therapy, and countless self-help strategies—finding this state of inner wholeness remains elusive.

This reality came into sharp focus for me one afternoon. As the warm glow of the late afternoon sun filled my office, its light filtering through the window and casting elongated shadows across the room, I found myself lost in quiet reflection, contemplating the elusive inner joy that so many seek, yet few seem to find. The peaceful calm of the evening settled around me—until the sharp ring of my phone broke the silence, jolting me from my thoughts. Curiosity stirred as I reached for the phone.

"Hello?" I greeted, my voice laced with pleasant surprise. The caller ID revealed it was Steven, a voice from the past. Years had passed since our last conversation. Back then, Steven had been a respected pastor in South Africa, a pillar of faith for many. But rumors had surfaced over the years, whispering of conflict and disillusionment. His relationship with a significant financial sponsor and the church leadership had deteriorated, leading not only to his resignation but to a personal crisis that shattered his marriage and completely upended the path he had once walked.

Steven's life had since spiraled into a whirlwind of indulgence and escapism. Drugs, especially cocaine, and a string of fleeting relationships had become central to his existence. Paradoxically, despite this chaotic lifestyle, his business acumen flourished, propelling him into the ranks of the affluent, where he spent his days rubbing shoulders with the nation's elite.

After the usual pleasantries and catching up, I felt a natural connection and cautiously broached the topic that weighed on my mind. "What happened, Steven?" I asked, my voice carrying a blend of concern and curiosity. His response came slowly, tinged with a deep melancholy that seemed to travel through the phone line. He began by recounting his childhood, growing up in a deeply committed Christian family, where he spent countless hours fully immersed in revival meetings. His father, a Pentecostal preacher, had risen to international fame, leading a megachurch and becoming a prominent figure in the Christian world.

Yet, beneath this outward display of spiritual strength lay a complex web of personal challenges and internal conflicts. Steven shared how, in his early years, his mother had left the family and became involved in a promiscuous lifestyle with both men and women, often doing drugs and having little to no contact with her children for many months at a time. Prior to this, his grandfather, once a respected pastor of a large evangelical church and a denominational leader, had tragically ended his own life, a casualty of his religion's harsh stigmas against homosexuality.

Steven's own journey into ministry was as rapid as it was turbulent. A divine call, experienced in a solitary moment of nature, had pulled him away from his university studies and led him to Bible college. His rise to the position of pastor was swift, but the path was littered with family discord and scandals. The final rupture came when tensions with the church leadership grew too great, leaving him embittered and disillusioned, and ultimately driving him away from the ministry altogether.

Steven's life, now fueled by escapism, became a desperate attempt to silence the mental unrest that had shadowed him for years. The indulgence in drugs and transient relationships wasn't so much about rebellion against his faith; it was an effort to numb the unresolved emotional pain that religion had failed to heal. He had tried to self-medicate the wounds of his fractured self-image and broken family history, only to find that material success brought no relief from the inner storm.

Now, his voice heavy with hard-earned wisdom, Steven spoke of the crumbling façade of his family's religious legacy. "God may well orchestrate the universe," he pondered, "but the path God supposedly laid out for my wellbeing failed me and much of my family, even though we were deeply committed Christians." Then, with stark clarity, Steven asserted, "It's just not working, and it's not due to a lack of sincerity or commitment."

As Steven reflected on the collapse of his ministry and personal life, it became clear that his disillusionment ran much deeper than just conflicts in his relationships—it was rooted in the unresolved trauma of his childhood and the hypocrisy and manipulation he had witnessed within religious circles. These wounds, left unhealed for so long, had slowly eroded his faith and sense of self, leaving him to grapple with the painful contradictions between the promised blessings of the message to which he had devoted his life and the harsh realities of his own experience. His outward success, while impressive, only masked the deep cracks in his wellbeing. Without a spiritual anchor that could truly sustain him, Steven found himself adrift, forced to face the mental unrest that had gradually overtaken his inner world.

Steven's story is not unique. All around the world, people are seeking answers. Whether they turn to religion, therapy, or other methods of self-improvement, many feel the same frustration—despite their best efforts, mental wellbeing remains elusive.

An Epidemic of Stress

In today's fast-paced world, the pressures we face seem to grow more intense with each passing day. We are constantly bombarded with information, demands, and expectations that leave little room for pause. The demands of work and family, the pressures of social media, and the constant stream of bad news can make it feel like we are always in survival mode. It's no wonder that stress, anxiety, and burnout have reached epidemic levels.

Consider this: 95% of American workers report feeling stressed on a daily basis, whether it's the pressure to meet deadlines, balance relationships, or simply stay afloat in a world that never stops moving.[1] It's not just about work anymore—many feel this pressure in every area of life. Parents feel the weight of raising children in an uncertain world. College students are overwhelmed with academic expectations and fears about the future. Social media bombards us with images of "perfect" lives, leaving many to feel like they're falling short, no matter what they do.

It's easy to feel trapped. Stress and anxiety don't just reside in our minds—they take a toll on our bodies, too. They show up as sleepless nights, chronic fatigue, headaches, and even long-term illnesses. The mind and body are interconnected, and when our mental wellbeing is compromised, our physical health often follows. In fact, studies have shown that chronic stress is a major contributor to heart disease, weakened immune systems, and a host of other health problems.

When we experience stress and anxiety, our bodies enter a state of heightened alert, often referred to as the "fight or flight" response. While this reaction can be useful in short bursts, chronic stress keeps our bodies in this state for extended periods, leading to harmful effects. Elevated cortisol levels, the hormone released during stress, can damage various bodily systems over time, impacting our cardiovascular and immune systems. Research has shown that chronic stress increases the risk of developing conditions like hypertension, diabetes, and even autoimmune diseases as the body becomes less capable of regulating inflammation and fighting off infections. This ongoing strain weakens our resilience, making us more susceptible to both physical and mental health issues.

For many, the solutions we've been taught to rely on— whether it's self-help books, religious faith, or even therapy—don't seem to provide lasting relief. We might find temporary moments of peace, but they often feel fleeting. We strive to keep up with life's demands, yet deep down, many of us feel like we're running on empty. We want more than just a quick fix. We crave something deeper—something that addresses the root of our stress and anxiety, not just the symptoms.

Despite the countless strategies we turn to, the reality is that mental health challenges are becoming more prevalent. Anxiety disorders are the most common mental illness in the United States, affecting over 40 million adults each year.[2] Depression is rising globally, and suicide rates have increased dramatically in many countries. Even those who appear to have it all together on the outside often wrestle with feelings of inadequacy, loneliness, or a sense that something fundamental is missing in their lives.

This struggle isn't limited to any one group of people. It touches the lives of everyone—from successful executives to young students, from stay-at-home parents to religious leaders. Many feel an internal dissonance—a gap between the life they're living and the life they long for, between how they present themselves to the world and the way they truly feel inside. This book aims to explore that very gap, offering a path toward lasting inner peace and mental wellbeing by drawing on both timeless wisdom and new science.

A Brief Overview

In the pages ahead, I want to share a profound truth with you: Peace, love, wisdom, creativity, and meaning aren't distant or hard to reach—they've been within you all along. Like the young shepherd in *The Alchemist*, who searched the world for treasure only to find it was at his starting point, we, too, have an inner dimension waiting to be uncovered.

To uncover this inner reality, we will draw on both ancient wisdom and modern science—including insights from Jesus, particularly those rooted in the original Aramaic language, quantum physics, neuroscience, neuro-cardiology, psychology, scriptures, and diverse spiritual traditions. Imagine a perspective where ancient teachings don't conflict with modern discoveries but instead complement one another. We'll explore how science can deepen our understanding of spiritual truths, helping us find a path to inner wholeness. This approach allows us to break free from the patterns of thought that keep us stuck in stress and anxiety, offering real tools to navigate life's challenges.

At the heart of Life Ascending is the idea that true elevation—true mental wellbeing—comes from a spiritual awakening. This awakening lifts us beyond the ego's limitations and lets us see life from a higher, more connected perspective. When we embrace this shift, we unlock a deep sense of peace that transforms how we view ourselves and the world. It enhances our mental health, strengthens our relationships, and helps create a more compassionate, interconnected world. This awakening also opens us up to universal wisdom and creativity, leading us to a deeper sense of purpose and fulfillment.

Chapter i, *A View from Above*, explores the fundamental question, "What is life?" and introduces the concept of the ascending life—a life that transcends ordinary existence to embody virtues such as inner peace and unconditional love. This ascending life is not about external achievements or success but rather an inner transformation that lifts us to a new state of awareness. Through this elevated perspective, we experience a profound shift in how we view ourselves and the world around us. Inner peace becomes our natural state, freeing us from anxiety and fear, while unconditional love flows effortlessly, transforming our relationships and interactions. These qualities have a ripple effect, reshaping how we navigate life's challenges, deepening our sense of purpose, and enriching our overall wellbeing.

Chapter 2, *The Chaos Within the Mind,* delves into the root causes of our mental unrest by examining the inner voices that shape our sense of wellbeing. Formed in childhood, these voices subtly influence our thoughts, emotions, and decisions as adults, leading to cycles of anxiety and inner conflict. As we grow, the judgments we make—about ourselves and others—fuel this mental chaos, preventing us from finding peace. This chapter uncovers how these internal narratives create dissonance and provides insights into unraveling the mental chaos many of us face.

Chapter 3, *Reshaping Our Reality,* explores the intricate connection between reality and perception, asking the crucial question: "Is it really possible to change our reality, and if so, how?" While some aspects of life may be beyond our control, our experiences are largely shaped by how we perceive and interact with reality. This chapter delves into transforming our reality, drawing on insights from quantum physics, empirical research, and the teachings of Jesus, with a focus on the transformative power of meditation.

Chapter 4, *Know Thy Self,* probes the existential question: "What am I?"—a deeper inquiry than "Who am I?" which relates to our personality or, as ancient texts describe it, the ego. This chapter seeks to uncover our true and deepest essence by examining consciousness as spirit from both scientific and ancient wisdom perspectives. We also explore the concept of *logos* as the organizing principle of existence, along with Jesus's declaration that we are the light of the world, illustrating how these ideas affirm our fundamental nature as spirit and consciousness.

Chapter 5, *The Vibrational Signature,* explores how our life experiences shape our state of being, creating a unique energy or spirit that others can sense. This chapter dives into the emerging field of neuro-cardiology, which shows the powerful connection between the heart and the brain and also examines Jesus's teachings on the kingdom of God. It invites us to awaken to the divine reality that permeates all things, to recognize the sacredness within ourselves and in all of life, and to live in alignment with this higher truth. By doing so, we begin to resonate with a deeper, more meaningful frequency that influences not only our own wellbeing but also the world around us.

Chapter 6, *The Barrier of the Ego*, examines the ego's impact on our lives, revealing how it generates pain, division, and inner turmoil, while standing as a major obstacle to cultivating a reality that enhances our wellbeing. The chapter also explores Paul's distinction between the ego and Christ, offering fresh insights into perspectives not often emphasized in traditional Christian teachings. By understanding how the ego limits our ability to experience inner peace and authentic connection, we can begin to dismantle its influence and open ourselves to a higher state of awareness where love, unity, and true wellbeing flourish.

Chapter 7, *Light on Shadows*, delves into the "inner shadows"—the parts of our personality that remain unconscious and hidden from our full awareness. These shadows consist of repressed emotions, subconscious fears, unresolved traumas, and unacknowledged desires, all of which obscure our perception of our true essence and the state of unconditioned consciousness. These hidden aspects often give rise to dysfunctional behavior and distorted thinking, shaping how we experience life without us even realizing it. To break free from these ingrained patterns, we explore the teachings of Jesus on the liberating power of knowing the truth.

Chapter 8, *Navigating Our Inner Maps*, explores the inherent biases and unconscious mental frameworks that serve as our internal navigation systems, shaping how we perceive and interact with the world. These cognitive maps are fluid and ever-changing, reflecting the evolving nature of our consciousness as it moves from being driven by ego and fear to embracing a state of unifying love. By understanding these inner maps, we can recognize how they influence our decisions and relationships and learn to reorient them toward a more harmonious and connected way of living.

Chapter 9, *The Heart as a Conduit*, examines how the heart serves as a bridge between the physical and spiritual dimensions of life, guiding us toward a state of inner peace and deep connection. This chapter delves into the ancient practice of meditation, tracing its roots across Eastern traditions and its presence in mystical Christian practices such as contemplation. It highlights how meditation helps us transcend the ego's noise, aligning our heart, mind, and soul with divine love and wisdom. By tapping into the heart's natural capacity for coherence, we can break free from the stress, anxiety, and disconnection that cloud our awareness, allowing us to experience life from a place of inner stillness and profound love.

Chapter 10, *The Melody Within,* introduces HeartFaith meditation as a practice to realign your heart, mind, and soul—like a luthier tuning a violin for harmony. The chapter explains how meditation helps us move beyond emotional and mental chaos, guiding us to the deeper peace and love within. By cultivating gratitude, peace, love, joy, and grace, HeartFaith meditation allows us to live with more clarity, purpose, and connection. It sharpens our focus, reduces stress, and strengthens our relationships, helping us flow with life's rhythms and align with a greater sense of ease and divine presence.

Chapter 11, *The Wisdom Within,* addresses the challenge of making wise decisions in the face of life's complexities. The chapter highlights the truth that wisdom isn't just about knowledge; it's about transcending ego, managing emotions, and gaining a broader perspective. Drawing from spiritual traditions and modern science, it shows how inner stillness allows wisdom to emerge, leading to clearer thinking and more thoughtful responses. The chapter also explores how wisdom unlocks creativity, helping us solve problems and approach life with greater openness. Through HeartFaith meditation, we learn to cultivate this wisdom, enabling us to navigate challenges with patience, nonjudgment, and insight, ultimately enriching our mental wellbeing and relationships.

Chapter 12, *A Life of Awe,* explores the experience of awe, a feeling that captures the heart of this book. Awe is a state of awareness that goes beyond the limits of intellect, connecting us to the vast mystery of life and our unity with the divine presence—God. In this chapter, we ask key questions: How can we bring this sense of awe into our everyday lives, cultivating inner peace and a deep love for all of existence? And how can we use our unique gifts and creativity to inspire awe in others, spreading more light and wonder in the world?

Before we jump into Chapter 1, there are a couple of things I want you to know. First, to protect privacy, I've changed the names and some details of individuals mentioned in this book, except for public figures and those who've given permission to be identified. In some cases, I've also combined different stories and experiences into one for clarity and better narrative flow.

Second, while this book presents a set of ideas, it's not intended to serve as the final word on any subject. Though the content includes scientific theories—some not yet conclusively proven—and subjective beliefs, the awareness of what I refer to as an inner presence reaches beyond thoughts and concepts. This may seem like a subtle distinction, but it becomes profoundly clear when you experience this inner presence for yourself. The words are simply pointers to a dimension beyond language. As you read, what truly matters is finding a spark that awakens something within you—an awakening that can heal, offer deep wisdom, and help you navigate life's complexities with clarity and insight.

1

A VIEW FROM ABOVE

I n 1998, I set foot for the first time in the African city of Tabora. Nestled in the center of Tanzania, this quaint town quickly captivated my heart, establishing a profound connection that drew me back over fifteen times. Initially, our trips to Tabora involved landing on a picturesque, hilly airstrip dotted with gravel. However, with the airstrip undergoing renovations for several years, we had to divert our route. This change led us to fly first to Mwanza, where we embarked on a grueling eight-hour drive, navigating some of the most demanding roads imaginable, to reach our final destination.

These roads, particularly battered after the rainy season, were marred by massive potholes, each telling a story of nature's relentless force. On these journeys, the harsh terrain tested my patience to its very edge, often sending me on an emotional rollercoaster between frustration and a sense of self-pity. I would often promise myself to never repeat that journey. Yet, as memories of the hardship faded in light of the work I felt compelled to do there, I found myself traveling that same road more times than I cared to admit—at least until 2014....

While surfing the internet, I stumbled upon a small airline primarily servicing mining engineers in the area. I reached out to them, and, to my relief, they agreed to arrange a stop in Tabora for only $180. It was an offer too good to pass up, so I promptly secured my ticket before they could reconsider.

Before long, I was seated beside the pilot in a twelve-seater Cessna, journeying alongside miners from Mwanza to Tabora. Elevated high above the ground, my entire perspective shifted. Gazing down at the roads winding through breathtaking landscape and charming country-side, my earlier frustrations and self-pity gave way to a sense of awe and gratitude.

Looking at the same terrain from this new height, the potholes that once dominated my attention receded into insignificance. This aerial viewpoint broadened my perception, allowing me to see the landscape as a cohesive whole, transcending its varied contours and unveiling a deeper harmony within nature.

This trip into the heart of Tanzania is a vivid metaphor for the trek we make through life. On this journey, there's not only the external world we can see and touch—defined by the tangible dimensions of time, space, and matter—but also an internal landscape filled with our thoughts, emotions, and imaginations. This inner realm profoundly influences how we perceive the external world, including ourselves and our environment.

Navigating Tanzania's rugged and hurdle-filled landscape mirrors an internally stressful life. Just as the road's obstacles can narrow our focus to the immediate challenges ahead, feelings such as frustration and despair can similarly confine our perspective, preventing us from seeing the beauty of the gift of life.

Think of those moments when life's anxieties press in— the relentless demands of our fast-paced world, the crushing weight of unmet expectations, the never-ending notifications on our devices. Like a road riddled with potholes, these pressures jolt us, stirring up a mix of emotions.

Perhaps you've wrestled with an inner critic—a voice that replays past mistakes and leaves you anxious about what lies ahead. This voice can cast a shadow over your brightest moments, magnifying insecurities and doubts. Then there's the scarcity mindset that creeps in, trapping us in a race for limited resources, always chasing more. This mentality spirals into stress, straining not just our peace of mind but also our relationships.

Fear is another powerful force, a lens that distorts our view of the world, making us see threats where none exist. Fear can paralyze us, keeping us from embracing life's opportunities due to fear of failure or rejection. And consider the moments when we hastily judge others, seeing them through the narrow lens of our preconceptions. These judgments stifle growth and create division, preventing us from contributing to a compassionate, more inclusive society.

Fortunately, there is another way to navigate life's journey. This path is marked by an inner peace, transcending fleeting thoughts and emotions, despite the external turbulence we may encounter. It's like switching to a higher level of travel—a metaphorical flight that frees us from the limitations of the ego and the narrow self-interest that so often keep us grounded. In this elevated state of awareness, life's difficulties appear smaller and less daunting, replaced by a profound sense of awe and connection with all of existence.

These dual experiences—ground-level versus aerial—challenge us to see that our inner world isn't simply a reaction to external events. It is shaped by powerful internal forces that determine how we perceive reality. Fearful thoughts may trap us in a limited, constricted view of life, but when we tap into inner peace and unconditional love, we transcend these barriers and catch a glimpse of a boundless reality full of potential for growth and unity.

In this light, the journey to Tabora becomes more than just a physical one—it's a metaphor for an inward journey, inviting us to reflect on the nature of our inner landscape and how profoundly it shapes our perception of the world. It asks us to consider: Will we remain prisoners of the potholes and obstacles along our path, or can we rise above them, embracing a more expansive, interconnected view of reality that's infused with love?

This chapter lays the foundation for what it means to navigate this transcendent path. Various spiritual traditions speak of this in terms like nonduality, higher consciousness, or awakening. In traditional Christianity, it's often called walking in the Spirit. Psychology offers a parallel concept in Abraham Maslow's hierarchy of needs, culminating in self-actualization and, ultimately, self-transcendence—what we might call higher consciousness.

As we explore the idea of an ascending life, it's natural to feel like it's unattainable—perhaps even too idealistic. I used to think the same. For years, I was skeptical of the lofty promises of a more fulfilling life. But I discovered I was wrong. It was in my most challenging moments that I began to uncover a path to deeper mental wellbeing. My hope is that as we embark on this journey together, you will find your way to an inner awakening that transcends anything we could ever put into words.

What's Life?

To understand the essence of "life ascending" and its powerful impact on our wellbeing, we first need to dive into what we really mean by life. Don't worry if this introduction feels a bit abstract and mystical at first—we'll keep returning to these concepts throughout the book, gradually showing how they relate to unlocking greater mental wellbeing.

Life is a word we all use, but it holds vastly different meanings for each of us. Most of the time, we view life through a biological lens—a collection of physical experiences within our human bodies. This everyday understanding of life is tied to our actions, emotions, and memories, all anchored in the physical world: our relationships, careers, and the natural beauty we witness.

Within this framework, life is finite, starting at birth and ending at death. We often think of life as a journey, assuming that when our bodies fail, life itself ceases to exist. The Greek word *bios* perfectly describes this kind of life—the tangible, biological existence we experience day to day. *Bios* reflects the physical life that is bound to the cycles of nature, much like the growth, flourishing, and decline we observe in plants, animals, and ecosystems. Life, from this viewpoint, is a temporary phenomenon, confined to time and space, and subject to the laws of nature. It follows the rhythms of birth and death, growth and withering, and reflects the transient nature of existence.

But many quantum physicists propose a view of life that challenges traditional ideas, suggesting that the deeper essence of life is consciousness. A particularly striking concept in quantum theory is the observer effect, which shows that particles exist in multiple wave states of probability until observed. This phenomenon has inspired theories suggesting that consciousness collapses these wave states into physical reality. Physicists like John Archibald Wheeler have built on this idea, proposing a *participatory universe,* where reality itself depends on conscious observation for its existence[1]—an intriguing concept that we will revisit and explore further later in the book for greater clarity and insight.

Similarly, the theory of biocentrism, developed by Dr. Robert Lanza, argues that life creates the universe, rather than the other way around. Lanza suggests that time, space, and even the physical world are constructs shaped by consciousness itself.[2] From this perspective, life is consciousness, because the universe, as we know it, only exists through the conscious awareness that brings it into being. This view challenges traditional, materialistic conceptions of life and proposes a deeper, more interconnected understanding of existence.

Particle physicist Heinrich Päs takes this idea one step further in his book The One. Päs argues that quantum mechanics reveals a deep sense of oneness in the cosmos, showing that everything we experience is part of a unified reality.[3] He suggests that consciousness is not an isolated phenomenon, but an integral part of this "One-Life." This means that both our individual consciousness and the fabric of reality itself are expressions or emanations of this all-encompassing One.

The brain and/or the heart might then act as receivers of consciousness that becomes localized in us. This view has been explored by others in the scientific field as well, such as Roger Penrose, who has proposed that consciousness arises from quantum processes within the brain's micro-tubules.[4] According to this theory, our conscious experience may be an expression of quantum phenomena that exist in the universe as a whole, again implying that our awareness is part of something far more expansive than the individual mind.

This idea isn't unique to modern science. For centuries, ancient mystical traditions—from Hinduism and Buddhism to Christianity and Judaism—have embraced the belief that the true essence of life is rooted in spirit or universal consciousness. Though these traditions use different language, they all converge on the same foundational truth: there exists a dimension beyond physical reality, a consciousness or life that is the Ground of Being and the Source from which all physical reality emerges.

Earlier we looked at the Greek word *bios* which represents life within time, space, and matter. In the Greek, there's another word for life: *zoe* – the eternal divine life that transcends the limitations of physical existence. The term eternal here doesn't refer to something that simply lasts forever within time, like the *bios* life. Instead, eternal in the context of *zoe* means timeless—a state of existence outside the boundaries of time, matter, and space.

In this understanding, *zoe life* is always present in the now because it doesn't follow the linear path of past, present, or future. It exists beyond the clockwork of time that governs our bios life. *Zoe life* is the essence of existence that is ever-present—not something that stretches endlessly into the future, but something that perpetually resides in the current moment.

This concept may be difficult to grasp at first because we're conditioned to think of eternity as something that unfolds across an infinite timeline. However, *zoe life* is a completely different reality. It isn't bound by the cycles of birth, decay, or death, and it doesn't fade or deteriorate. *Zoe* simply is—pure consciousness, divine presence, and life in its truest form.

The Bible points to this deeper reality that undergirds the physical realm when it says, "In [God] we live, move, and have our being,"[5] emphasizing our profound connection to a transcendent presence. Paul reinforces this idea by stating, "God is above all, and through all, and in all,"[6] highlighting how God's presence permeates every aspect of life—God as the One-Life and infinite consciousness that unites and sustains all.

Taking this even further, Paul expresses his desire for the heart and the deeper mind (subconscious) to be illuminated to the truth that "Christ is all and in all."[7] This speaks to a transformative awakening—one that reveals that our true nature is not limited to the physical form but is an emanation of the divine consciousness that fills the universe.

An important biblical concept that deepens the understanding of zoe-life as consciousness is the connection between life and light. The Bible states that "...life (zoe) is the light..."[8] and refers to God as both life and light. So, if light equates with life, what about light defines this life? Light illuminates reality, and similarly, consciousness is what allows us to perceive and understand reality. In other words, life and consciousness are intertwined—just as light reveals what is hidden, consciousness brings awareness and clarity to the nature of existence.

However, just as light comes in varying degrees of intensity that affect how much we can see, so too does consciousness come in different levels of awareness. Jesus highlighted this when he said, "you are light of the world." He also spoke about how our minds have been darkened because we do not walk fully in the light. What does this mean? It suggests that we are unaware of our true essence as consciousness because we are trapped within the limitations of our minds, perceiving reality only through the lenses of time, space, and matter.

In a sense, we live confined by the mind's thoughts and emotions, rarely present in the now and unaware of the zoe-life that exists within us. We miss the deeper reality that God is not distant but within us, and that we are part of the One-Life, the true essence of our being. Without this awareness, we remain in a kind of mental darkness, constantly seeking external validation or future achievements to feel fulfilled.

So, what is the ascending life? It is awakening to consciousness as our true self. It's becoming aware of the peaceful and loving presence within—the silent "I am"—and recognizing its oneness with the Source. Spiritual traditions suggest that our minds have been clouded, but as the light of consciousness breaks through, we awaken to a deeper connection with the One-Life. This awakening is essential for our mental wellbeing and lies at the heart of what it means to live the ascending life.

Increasingly, science shows that practices like meditation help us cultivate awareness of the present moment, aligning with the idea of awakening to consciousness as our true self. By quieting the mind and tuning into the now, we reconnect with the deeper essence of life and foster greater mental clarity and wellbeing.

Finding Life's Essence in Stillness

The questions now become: what are the characteristics of this ascending life or higher consciousness? How can we know when we are truly touching the essence of life—the *zoe-life*?

We begin with the foundation of the ascending life—inner stillness. Words alone cannot capture the true essence of this stillness, for it is neither a concept nor a thought. This is why spiritual texts and sages often describe it as mystical. No language can fully express it, and no set of beliefs can contain it. At best, words can only point in its direction.

Throughout this book, I will use words as signposts, guiding you toward this inner dimension. But true understanding comes from awakening to it—beyond the limitations of language, beyond words themselves.

What is this stillness? It is the inner space in which our existence is perceived, giving rise to thoughts and experiences.

Think of it as the canvas upon which the artwork of life is painted—without it, there would be no experience, no perception, no life as we know it. This stillness is pure, unfiltered awareness—the foundation of everything that follows.

At its core, this stillness is inseparable from your true essence. It is the "I am" that transcends your personality and physical form—a presence beyond the reach of the senses, existing outside the boundaries of space and time.

When you touch this stillness, you let go of the egoic self —the part of you tied to worldly concerns and temporary identities. In doing so, you encounter your true self, aligning with the timeless truth that Jesus referenced: "You are in this world, but not of this world."[9] While the world is made of matter, your essential nature—your spirit, consciousness, or awareness of being—is beyond the physical, and it is inseparable from this stillness.

This inner stillness is not the absence of noise, nor is it void of content. Instead, it is the intelligence from which all creation arises—the underlying consciousness that forms the bedrock of everything.

Ask yourself: how could this possibly be separate from who you are? It can't be, because it is the formless essence from which your physical form has emerged. It sustains you—it is the very source of life itself.

To return to this inner state of stillness is to return to the beginning—a kind of rebirth, where you become aware of awareness itself. It is the starting point for seeing and entering what Jesus called the kingdom of God.

This stillness is always present, always here and now. It cannot be found in the past or the future because it exists outside time. It is timeless. To become aware of this timeless dimension is simply to tune into the present moment.

For instance, when you immerse yourself in the simplicity of nature—a tree standing tall, a flower in bloom—you can access a deep inner stillness. In this state of pure awareness, you touch the essence of life ascending. This stillness is not of this world, has no form, yet it is the truest expression of who you are.

As we delve deeper into the essence of this transformational path, we see that it all begins here—with a return to inner stillness. This is the starting point, the foundation upon which actual mental wellbeing is built. Reconnecting with this pure awareness, untouched by the world yet deeply connected to the essence of life itself, is the first step in rising above the challenges of everyday life.

Unconditional Love: Seeing Through the Lens of Oneness

From the depths of inner stillness arises a profound sense of love—a feeling of oneness with all things. This connection is so deep that it dissolves the boundaries between you and the world around you. As I gazed out of the airplane window, the once-disjointed bumps and potholes of the road below blended into a seamless whole. What seemed fragmented and imperfect from the ground became unified and harmonious when viewed from above. Similarly, unconditional love transcends the imperfections and separations we often perceive in relationships, revealing the inherent oneness of all things.

To truly understand love, we must recognize that it can take many forms depending on the state of consciousness from which it arises. On the one hand, there is transactional love—the type of love most common in our everyday lives—while on the other, there is unconditional or divine love, which emerges from a deeper, more elevated state of being.

Transactional love operates like a calculated exchange, much like a vending machine: you offer kind words, thoughtful actions, or gifts with the expectation of receiving something in return—be it affection, support, or validation. But when the "transaction" fails to meet these expectations, frustration and resentment often arise.

At its core, transactional love stems from a deeper, unspoken fear: the fear of being alone, the fear of rejection, and the fear of not being enough. These fears shape a love that is not freely given but instead driven by the need to protect ourselves from vulnerability. In this dynamic, love becomes conditional—a mask we wear to secure our own emotional needs rather than a true expression of unconditional care for another.

Consider the relationship between a parent and child. When a parent's affection becomes overly possessive or controlling, it reflects fear—fear of loss or separation— rather than unconditional love. Despite the parent's belief that this is unconditional love, it operates on transactional terms, creating cycles of mental anguish and suffering. Over time, unmet expectations lead to disappointment and resentment in the mother, leaving her feeling unloved and unappreciated, while the child, overwhelmed by the weight of these demands, seeks to escape—emotionally or physically—further straining the relationship.

In contrast, imagine a parent who loves their child simply because the child exists. There is no demand for gratitude, no expectation that the child fulfills a role or an image. This is unconditional love. Like the sun, it shines freely and equally on all, asking nothing in return, simply radiating warmth and light because it is its nature to do so.

Unconditional love feels like a deep sigh after holding your breath for too long. It is the peace that comes when you stop trying to earn love and realize that love flows effortlessly, freely, from the stillness within you. At its core, unconditional love is untainted by fear, free from the shackles of obligations and expectations. It is inherently kind and compassionate, emerging naturally from the depths of our being.

When Jesus taught, "love your neighbor as yourself,"[10] he wasn't suggesting we love others as much as ourselves, but rather that we see and love the neighbor as an extension of our own being. This profound insight reflects the essence of unconditional love—a love that dissolves the illusion of separateness and reveals the inherent unity of all life.

Just as my view from the airplane allowed me to see the landscape below in a new light, transcending the bumps and rough terrain, unconditional love allows us to rise above the limitations of transactional love. It opens our hearts to the oneness of all life, inviting us to experience love in its purest, most expansive form.

Imagine the freedom of loving without fear, expectation, or obligation. Unconditional love lifts the weight of demands and allows us to embrace others as they are. It is not a love that binds—it is a love that liberates. When we awaken to the stillness of our being, we discover that true love has no conditions, no demands—it simply flows. This love is already within you, waiting to be shared freely with the world.

The Heart: Gateway to Unconditional Love

Across spiritual traditions, love is often depicted as a divine essence, flowing like a timeless river through the heart. This heart, transcending its biological function, symbolizes our inner sanctum—a sacred space where feelings, intuition, and higher wisdom converge. It serves as a conduit for divine love, opening a gateway to a deeper understanding of ourselves and the universe.

This understanding of the heart's role is also deeply rooted in the language and teachings of Jesus. In Aramaic, the word *naphsha* refers to the small or individual self— the soul. The *naphsha*-self enables us to experience life through a personal lens, confined within the boundaries of space and time. In contrast, the word *ruha* signifies the universal spirit or *zoe-life*, the essence of "I-ness" that flows freely, eternally connected to the source of reality—*Alaha* in Aramaic.[11] Unlike the *naphsha*, the *ruha*-Self transcends time and space, representing the infinite breath or consciousness.

Although *ruha* and *naphsha* appear distinct, they are not separate. They are interconnected in the same way as the air we breathe—simultaneously universal and personal. This connection finds its embodiment in the heart, or *leba* in Aramaic. The heart was understood as more than a physical organ; it was considered the seat of knowing and feeling, embodying love and peace but also fear and shame. It symbolized the shared field between the individual self (*naphsha*) and the universal spirit (*ruha*) or infinite consciousness, shaping how we perceive and interact with reality.

When the heart was whole—open and free from fear— the *ruha* flowed unhindered, and the *naphsha*-self experienced reality as unified, giving rise to profound inner peace, love, and joy. But when the heart was fractured— closed off by shame and fear—it lost awareness of the inherent oneness of all creation. In this state, the heart became consumed by the illusion of separation, leaving the self trapped in ego and disconnected from the divine unity that pervades all things.

A word that illuminates the connection between unconditional love and this understanding of the heart is *chesed* in ancient Hebrew. *Chesed* embodies kindness, love, and infinite grace flowing from the divine Spirit through the heart into our soul. It enriches our lives and deepens our connection with God and creation.

To truly grasp this idea, imagine sitting quietly in your backyard at sunset, watching the colors of the sky melt into one another. In that stillness, as distractions fade, you may feel a deep peace rising within you, blossoming into love and gratitude for life. Awe and wonder awaken—a quiet energy flowing, unburdened by fear. This fleeting moment mirrors the essence of *chesed*: divine love coursing through the heart, bringing with it a sense of infinite grace.

Recent scientific studies suggest that this spiritual understanding of the heart might have a basis in physical reality. The heart, it turns out, is not just a mechanical pump but an organ of remarkable complexity and intelligence. It generates the body's most powerful electromagnetic field, which changes in response to our emotions.

When our inner self aligns with deep love, gratitude, and peace, the heart's electromagnetic field becomes more coherent and harmonious. This state, known as "heart coherence," has been linked to numerous benefits, including improved cognitive function, enhanced immune response, and an overall sense of wellbeing.

The heart communicates with the brain and the rest of the body not only through the nervous system but also through this electromagnetic field. When we feel love, the heart sends signals to the brain that can trigger the release of chemicals like oxytocin, often called the "love hormone." Intriguingly, the heart's electromagnetic field extends outward, creating an interactive space where our internal state resonates with the external environment. This suggests that our inner wellbeing can influence and be influenced by the energies and emotions of those around us, highlighting our profound interconnectedness.

These scientific insights and the intuitive wisdom of spiritual traditions converge on a singular idea: Unconditional love is a unifying force that flows through the heart. Whether we view the heart as a spiritual center or a physical organ with electromagnetic influence, its role in the experience and expression of love is undeniable. Understanding the heart gives us a glimpse into the multidimensional nature of love —an energy, a feeling, and a unifying connection.

Thus, as we reflect on how we perceive reality and experience life, we must consider the energies that fuel our views of ourselves and the world around us. Our outlook on life expands as our hearts resonate more with love and peace. We become more secure, peaceful, and hopeful. The anxieties of tomorrow, along with old regrets and fears of scarcity, fade into the background, losing their power over us, much like the potholes and rough terrain that once seemed daunting from the ground but became almost invisible from the sky.

The Truth that Lifts Us Higher

I don't often dwell on the past, but I recognize its value in giving context to this idea of an elevated inner state. With that in mind, I want to briefly share how my journey led me to this point and how this book came to be.

It's often said that the truth sets us free. Many interpret this as a call to live with integrity, where honesty in our words and actions helps us release the weight of deceit. And it's true—there is a profound freedom in being true to our word and in our actions. Another way to view the truth that sets us free is to see it as aligning our inner feelings with our outer reality. This means expressing who we are and what we believe without hiding behind a facade. When we live authentically, caring less about external judgments, we harmonize our inner and outer worlds.

Without a doubt, living our truth and embodying integrity can enhance our sense of wellbeing. However, the initial thrill of authenticity often fades. We find ourselves slipping back into familiar patterns of negative thinking. Despite changes in our worldview and the way we interact with the world, underlying feelings such as stress, anxiety, worry, and resentment persist. These negative thought patterns can ensnare us once again. Consequently, we seek guidance from therapists, psychologists, and religious leaders in our ongoing quest for psychological freedom and wellbeing.

The phrase "the truth sets you free" originates from Jesus's words, "You shall know the truth, and the truth shall set you free."[12] Many Christians interpret "truth" as having a correct mental concept of God that aligns with their particular understanding of the Bible. This belief can lead to a sense of spiritual superiority, where their faith is viewed as the only true path, implying that they alone possess the truth. The reasoning often follows: Since my Christian faith is the truth, and I am a Christian, I must fully know the truth.

Yet, Jesus claimed that knowing the truth would liberate us. If, despite our faith, we remain entangled in negative thoughts and actions, it suggests that we may not fully grasp the truth he spoke of. In other words, the most reliable sign of truly "knowing the truth" is its power to transform our wellbeing. Does it bring relief from stress, anxiety, worry, and depression? Does it lead to a peace that surpasses understanding, guiding us toward a life that is genuinely fulfilling and meaningful?

This quest for the truth that Jesus referenced became deeply personal for me in 2008, during a period of overwhelming stress and feelings of inadequacy. As a minister, I had the privilege of speaking in some of the largest churches in the world and leading large-scale campaigns across many parts of the globe. My ministry encompassed various leadership roles, including lead pastor, Bible college president, and ministerial fellowship head. Despite what many would view as significant accomplishments, I still found myself ensnared by persistent thoughts of stress, worry, and guilt and feelings of shame.

Amid this intense inner turmoil, which strained my relationships, career, and wellbeing, I quietly whispered these words one morning while gazing out a window at a canyon: "If there is a truth that can set me free, I want to know it." Until then, I had believed that my evangelical interpretation of Christianity represented that truth. However, the dissonance I was suffering hinted at an overlooked aspect of this truth.

Briefly, I experienced a sense of peace as I opened my heart to the possibility of true freedom. But soon, fear crept in, echoing the words I'd often heard: "Never doubt your beliefs. Guard yourself against deception. Beware of straying from the path."

Fear momentarily immobilized me, making me question if I was on the brink of a grave mistake. Reflecting on it, I realize that religious structures often veer toward self-preservation. My apprehensions were molded by a framework that thrives on uniformity. Any deviation or questioning can lead to shaming or exclusion. Yet, the depth of my struggle overshadowed my fears. I desired inner wholeness, and I realized that the path to that freedom required me to set aside preconceived notions, challenge long-held beliefs, and embrace the possibility of change based on new insights and discoveries.

This shift wasn't necessarily about discarding my faith but allowing my beliefs to be measured by the inner freedom they brought me. If faith doesn't bring the profound peace it promises, a peace surpassing all understanding, then we must question its value. It's one thing to experience love, passion, and kindness within the supportive embrace of like-minded individuals. But what about those quiet, solitary moments when we face the day-to-day challenges, armed only with our personal thoughts and struggles? And what about those times when we find ourselves in conflict, feeling the tension strain our relationships? If our spirituality doesn't work for us in such particular moments, how can we genuinely advocate its virtues to others?

A pivotal moment in my search for the truth that would set me free happened on a golf course on the outskirts of Toronto. Looking for direction, clarity, and private time for reflection, I went to a course I knew would not be busy and booked a tee time when no one else was around.

Standing with my driver in my hand on the first tee box, I noticed a gentleman by himself, sinking his putt to finish the first hole, almost 500 yards away from me. I deliberately took my time on that first hole, so he could get a head start on the second hole, safely ahead of me, and there would be no pressure to play with him (which I did not want to do).

About ten minutes later, I arrived at the second hole tee box and noticed the same man sitting on a bench, waiting for me. He introduced himself as Nick and asked if we could play together. Everything within me wanted to say no, but that would be rude, so I reluctantly agreed. Then I thought, "If I'm not getting any time for quiet reflection on the golf course, at least I can share my beliefs with him and get him converted."

For the next few hours, I shared what I believed with him. But something strange happened while I bombarded him with my worldview. Nick's manner of speaking was so different than mine. He didn't quote scriptures or share his beliefs with me. For him, having a set of thoughts we regard as the ultimate truth does not make us spiritual, regardless of what those beliefs may be. I couldn't comprehend it.

At the same time, there was such peace, patience, joy, kindness, compassion, generosity, and love about this man that I was utterly taken aback. How could he manifest these attributes if he didn't share my beliefs? It wasn't that he opposed my views. Instead, his connection with God— or whatever name you prefer to describe that which transcends all—appeared to be rooted in something beyond dogma, stories, and beliefs.

Something just made Nick so alive—something that went beyond all thoughts and mental constructs. I left that round of golf confused because, despite all my theological knowledge and ability to skillfully present what I believed, it felt like this man made a more significant impact on me than I did on him.

As time passed, I often mused over my unexpected meeting with Nick on the golf course. I wondered why so much of my spiritual life had been defined by rigid adherence to certain religious texts. It seemed as though words, concepts, and the "right" beliefs were essential to my understanding of faith, as if everything depended on aligning my thoughts with a specific doctrine. But what if God cannot be confined by these words and concepts, which are ultimately just creations of the brain? What if God exists beyond this dimension, beyond the mental frameworks we construct to understand reality? If that's true, then perhaps the virtues of peace and unconditional love reveal the divine essence more accurately than any doctrine or belief system could ever encapsulate.

That day, as I shared my beliefs with Nick, I was convinced I offered him the key to freedom. Yet, paradoxically, Nick seemed the "freer spirit." My soul, in contrast, didn't mirror the peace, grace, and love that seemed to radiate effortlessly from him.

Of course, I didn't know what internal struggle Nick might have been dealing with, but there was calmness and compassion in him that I had rarely seen before. I found myself wondering whether my religious beliefs had cut me off from the spiritual dimension within me. Had I taken scriptures and turned them into neatly packaged belief systems that merely bolstered my sense of self? Was my identity so entwined with a set of fixed thoughts that I found myself trapped within my own mind, completely oblivious to a divine dimension deep within me? Could this be why I felt so unfree? For a long time, these questions weighed heavily on my heart, leaving me feeling isolated and tormented by an internal struggle I couldn't escape.

It wasn't until I went through a series of personal crises—anger, resentment, guilt, and physical pain—that I finally turned inward. Feeling desperate, I sought stillness through meditation, and almost immediately, I became aware of a peaceful and loving presence within me—an experience I describe more fully in Chapter 3.

To my amazement, the physical pain I had endured for so long vanished within minutes. As I continued to meditate and immerse myself in this space of inner peace and love, my perception of reality began to shift. The mental and emotional turbulence that had once defined me started to dissipate, replaced by a profound sense of peace and freedom.

This internal shift sparked a deep curiosity: What was this inner presence? It felt like a tranquil space of stillness where the usual inner chatter—the voice in my head—was quieted, leaving only a pure awareness of being. Initially, I found it challenging to articulate what had happened. Driven to understand and describe my experiences, I immersed myself in the study of science, ancient and contemporary spiritual thoughts, psychology, and history.

It soon became evident that my experience was far from unique. Mystics, scientists, psychologists, philosophers, and modern spiritual teachers have all described similar experiences. I then began to explore the teachings of Jesus through the lens of his native Aramaic language and Semitic culture. Understanding Jesus's wisdom within that context often contrasted sharply with the interpretations I had encountered in my church background. More importantly, these studies illuminated not only my own experiences but also how we might all experience inner wholeness—a liberation from our mental suffering and collective pain.

The Invitation

My story may be different from yours, or perhaps similar, but regardless of your background, I hope this book will serve as a guide for you. As we embark on a path toward a fulfilling and authentic life, I find Rumi's words particularly inspiring: "Yesterday I was clever, so I wanted to change the world. Today, I am wise, so I am changing myself."[13] By turning our attention inward, we unlock the transformative power to reshape not only our inner life but also the world around us, leading us to a more profound sense of spiritual and mental wellbeing.

Now, let's turn our focus to the root cause of our mental unrest—the very thing that keeps us from experiencing the *zoe-life* through inner stillness, unconditional love, and a deepened sense of oneness.

2

THE CHAOS WITHIN THE MIND

Matthew Turner was the kind of man people admired. At thirty-eight, he had climbed the ranks of the corporate world with a steady determination that left colleagues in awe. He was the youngest vice president at a prominent financial firm.

Outside of work, Matthew's life seemed equally enviable. He had a beautiful home in an affluent suburb. His wife, Sarah, was the quintessential partner—intelligent, warm, and loving. They had two children, Lily and Jack, who were the center of their world. On weekends, you could find Matthew coaching Jack's little league team or attending Lily's ballet recitals, always present, always the picture of a devoted father.

To anyone on the outside looking in, Matthew was a man who had it all. But beneath the polished surface of Matthew's life was a man slowly unraveling, caught in a downward spiral fueled by the relentless voices in his head—voices that had haunted him for as long as he could remember.

It started in his childhood, which was shaped by a complex and often painful relationship with his parents, particularly his father, James Turner. James was a stern, stoic man, but beneath his rigid exterior lay a darkness that haunted the Turner household—James was an alcoholic. As a child, Matthew learned quickly to navigate the volatile environment his father's drinking created. He could always tell what kind of evening it would be by how his father's car pulled into the driveway. If the car screeched to a halt, tires crunching on gravel, Matthew's heart would race, knowing that the night would be filled with tension and the unpredictable wrath of a man who was both his father and a stranger.

James was a man of few words when sober, but alcohol loosened his tongue in the worst possible ways. He would berate Margaret, Mathew's mother, with cruel, cutting insults, tearing down her every effort to keep the household together. And then he'd turn to Matthew, his rage boiling over, laced with curses, and his voice dripping with disgust as he shouted, "You're nothing—worthless. You'll never be anything but a damn disappointment."

These words, slurred and angry, became a part of Matthew's internal dialogue. The inner critical voice that plagued him in adulthood was born on those nights, echoing the bitter words his father spat in drunken rages.

As much as Matthew feared James, he also craved his approval. He would go to great lengths to please his father, hoping that if he did everything right, the man would finally see him, not as a failure, but as a son worthy of pride.

If his father was a wall of stoicism and anger, his mother was a bundle of nerves. Margaret's life revolved around keeping the house in order and trying to anticipate the needs of her husband and son. But underneath her meticulous housekeeping was an undercurrent of anxiety that she tried, and often failed, to hide.

This constant state of anxiety became ingrained in Matthew's psyche. He internalized his mother's fear, which became another voice in his head, warning him of potential dangers. It was as if he had absorbed her anxiety, and it grew alongside the other voices that would later dominate his life.

When Matthew met Sarah in college, it felt like a reprieve from the oppressive atmosphere of his childhood. Sarah was everything Matthew's parents were not—warm, compassionate, and open-hearted. In the early years of their marriage, Sarah's warmth seemed to balance Matthew's more reserved nature. She encouraged him to relax, to take time for himself, and to enjoy the life they were building together. But as Matthew's career advanced, the voices in his head grew louder and more demanding. The pressure to succeed, to be the best at everything he did, became overwhelming.

The perfectionist's voice drove him to work long hours, striving to provide the best for his family. However, it also meant that he was rarely present, even when he was physically home. Sarah would try to talk to him, to draw him out, but Matthew was always distracted, his mind occupied by the next task that needed to be done.

As the years passed, another voice in his head began to undermine his confidence in his marriage. It whispered that Sarah would one day realize she had married the wrong man and would see through his facade and leave him. Matthew became increasingly withdrawn, convinced that any display of vulnerability would only accelerate the inevitable end.

The strain began to show in other areas of Matthew's life. At work, his obsession with perfection and fear of being exposed led to missed deadlines and a growing list of unfinished projects. He was paralyzed by indecision, terrified that any action he took would be the wrong one.

One evening, after a particularly stressful day at work, Matthew came home to find that Sarah had forgotten to pick up his dry cleaning. It was a small thing that normally wouldn't have mattered, but in his state of mind, it felt like the world was crumbling. The inner critical voice flared up, telling him this was just another example of how his life was out of control.

"Why can't you do anything right?" he snapped at her, his voice harsher than he intended. The look on Sarah's face

—a mix of hurt and confusion—was like a punch to the gut, but even as he saw it, he couldn't stop himself.

Matthew stormed out of the room, his heart pounding, the voices in his head louder than ever. They berated him for his outburst, calling him a failure as a husband, a man who couldn't even keep his own emotions in check. But at the same time, they justified his anger, telling him that Sarah should have known better and wasn't holding up her end of the bargain.

As such incidents piled up, Sarah began to withdraw as well. She no longer tried to talk to him about his day or feelings; instead, they fell into a pattern of avoidance. Conversations became brief and superficial, revolving around logistics rather than emotions. The warmth that once defined their relationship was slowly replaced by a cold, uncomfortable distance.

Desperate for answers, Matthew began to ask himself, *How do I escape these voices? How can I reclaim my life and transform my mental wellbeing?* He knew the first step was to dig deep and uncover the root cause of his mental unrest. Where did these voices come from? What had given them so much power that they now threatened everything—his marriage, his relationship with his children, and even his own identity?

Voices in Our Heads

When we think about inner voices, our minds often jump to extreme cases like Matthew's, whose life spirals into torment from an overwhelming internal dialogue. But the truth is, we all have voices in our heads—whispers, echoes, or sometimes, a steady stream of chatter. Whether or not we realize it, we carry on these internal conversations all day. A recent study reveals that we can sometimes talk to ourselves at a speed equivalent to 4,000 words per minute.[1]

At times, this rapid-fire conversation happening right inside our minds mimics the voices of people in our lives, turning their words over and over in our heads. Sometimes, we address ourselves directly, saying "you" like we're giving advice to someone else. And then there may be moments when we speak our own name in the third person—an act which, studies show, can actually guard against anxiety and improve our performance by creating a sense of separation between our deeper self and the constant chatter in our minds. This supports the timeless wisdom discussed in the last chapter: our true self is not our thoughts or emotions but something more profound and enduring.

Most of the time, this dialogue serves a purpose. It helps us weigh our options, nudging us toward the best decision, like an invisible advisor sorting through the pros and cons of life's dilemmas. But the nature of these inner voices is not always so helpful. The voices may ramble endlessly or engage in a full-blown dialogue within our mind, like an ongoing debate between our better angels and inner critics. More often than not, it feels like we do not control what the voices say. It's as if we're listening to a running commentary on our lives, not fully authoring it.

And sometimes, this voice turns against us. It replays the past like a broken record, forcing us to relive mistakes and regrets. It fixates on painful emotions, amplifying our fears and insecurities until they paralyze us. It whispers cruel things we'd never say aloud, sabotaging our peace of mind and pushing us toward self-destructive decisions. In those moments, the inner dialogue isn't just background noise—it's a relentless force that can make us feel trapped in our own thoughts, battling a voice we didn't ask for.

While reflecting on the mental unrest and inner suffering that so many people face, I came across a fascinating study by Polish psychologist Małgorzata Puchalska-Wasyl. She has done extensive research on internal dialogues and focuses on the different types of "inner voices" we experience, which play a crucial role in shaping our self-talk and influencing how we process thoughts.

Puchalska-Wasyl identified four main types of inner voices that emerge in these dialogues: the Faithful Friend, a voice that offers support and encouragement; the Ambivalent Parent, which mixes care with criticism; the Proud Rival, a competitive voice that pushes us to prove ourselves; and the Helpless Child, a voice of self-pity.[2]

When one of these inner voices becomes too dominant and forceful, it can deeply affect our mental wellbeing. For instance, if a critical or competitive voice takes over, it can increase levels of stress, anxiety, and self-doubt, leaving us feeling constantly inadequate or pressured to prove ourselves. On the other hand, when the voice of self-pity becomes overpowering, it can lead to feelings of helplessness, fear, and insecurity. This overwhelming sense of vulnerability can foster feelings of worthlessness, potentially spiraling into depressive states where we feel incapable of managing life's challenges.

How Childhood Echoes in Our Minds

The voices we hear in our heads are shaped by a complex web of factors unique to each person. While everyone's inner dialogue differs, there are key influences that determine whether or not these voices lead to mental unrest and inner suffering. Let's focus on a couple of these core elements.

One major factor is rooted in childhood experiences. For example, Matthew's story shows how the emotional dynamics of his early years directly shaped the inner voices that haunted him later in life.

These formative experiences extend beyond what we consciously remember, reaching back to our earliest days. Even before our brains developed the capacity for logical or creative thought, and long before we could form lasting episodic memories—those conscious recollections of events—we were immersed in a world of feelings.

From the moment of birth, we began absorbing sensations: the warmth of a caregiver's embrace, the pangs of hunger, the comforting touch of a gentle hand. These experiences were the first language we understood, a language not of words but of raw emotions. Simple actions, like being held or fed, brought pleasure, while hunger or discomfort introduced distress.

Your young brain began to make sense of the world by cataloging these experiences and searching for patterns to guide your responses. Take the infant's cry, for instance. It may have started as a spontaneous sound but evolved into a learned response. You discovered that crying often brought relief, not because of the cry itself, but due to the resulting care and attention from those around you. This nurturing response, filled with affection, became synonymous with comfort and the alleviation of distress.

As you grew, you began associating the most profound sense of comfort and joy with the feeling of being loved. The more you were enveloped in this love and care, the more prominent these pleasant feelings became, morphing into a pervasive sense of contentment. This contentment created a positive cycle: Your joyful expressions often brought even more attention and affection, reinforcing a loop that taught your brain about life's most essential values: love, contentment, and happiness.

These feelings became more than abstract ideas. They became a compass for navigating life. They guided your self-talk, shaped how you perceived the world, influenced your experiences, and directed your choices. Over time, these deeply embedded feelings didn't just affect your reality; they actively constructed it. The life you lead today, with its intricate myriad of memories, beliefs, and emotions, can be traced back to these foundational experiences and the patterns they set in motion within your brain.

Now, consider a different upbringing in a home where consistent care was lacking or distressing feelings weren't adequately addressed. As a child, you were vulnerable, reliant on the care and attention of your parents, primarily your mother, to nourish you. The unpleasant sensation of a dirty diaper needed their intervention, and their comforting touch was what settled your restless mind into sleep.

When this attention wasn't consistently provided, your mind internalized a deep sense of insecurity about the world. This insecurity sparked feelings of fear, leading your mind to develop various coping strategies to navigate these unsettling emotions. As you grew older, these unresolved feelings could manifest as anger, withdrawal, aggression, or even a passive acceptance of life's difficulties. These coping mechanisms didn't arise randomly— they reflect the dominant voices in your head, shaped by early experiences of instability or neglect. The angry voice, the fearful voice, or the voice that urges retreat are all attempts to protect you from the painful emotions rooted in childhood.

Conversely, even in a nurturing environment, life's unpredictable twists—like rejection, unmet parental expectations, or the pain of divorce—can add new layers of negative emotions. These experiences shape the voices in your head, embedding fear, self-doubt, or the presence of a harsh inner critic. Long after the events have passed, the fear of reliving such emotional pain often drives your inner dialogue, becoming a compass that influences not just your actions but also which voices dominate. Whether it's insecurity, self-blame, or caution, these voices, molded by both early and later emotional experiences, guide the way you engage with the world—and yourself.

You might wish to silence these voices or escape the constant loop of negative thoughts, but they persist because our most unsettling experiences are imprinted in our subconscious as patterns. These deeply embedded emotional memories continue to influence how we perceive the world, even when we can't consciously recall them. Like a hidden program running in the background of the mind, these subconscious patterns shape our self-perception, guide our tendencies, filter the information we're drawn to, and influence our thoughts—those inner voices—about reality and the world around us.

The Spectrum of Fear

At the root of subconscious patterns lies fear, a force that divides and isolates us, creating invisible boundaries between ourselves and others. While love unites and fosters connection, fear does the opposite—it fragments our relationships and builds barriers. Every negative emotion we experience—whether it's anger, jealousy, anxiety, resentment, or hatred—can be traced back to this underlying fear. Over time, fear hijacks the voices in our heads, turning them into its messengers, amplifying our insecurities, and reinforcing the emotional walls that keep us separated from one another.

Many spiritual teachings propose that the root of fear lies within the ego, a mental construct of self. Seen through the ego's lens, we perceive ourselves as isolated entities, separate from the rest of existence. This perceived separation fosters an "us versus them" mindset, in which anything external to our form—our "self" as the physical and psychological identity tied to the body and mind—appears different and frequently as a potential threat.

It leads us to view others with suspicion, as potential adversaries, who might not have our best interests at heart. This perspective naturally leads to conflict. Motivated by fear, we guard our personal space, beliefs, or sense of self against what we perceive as dangers. This defensive approach colors our interactions, transforming even the most harmless exchanges into arenas of potential conflict.

As the chasm of separation widens, it profoundly shapes our life experiences. Our horizons of understanding and empathy begin to narrow, and we start to view the world through an increasingly limited lens, tinged with suspicion. Influenced by "me against the world" inner voices, this limited viewpoint weakens our ability to truly understand and deeply connect with others, paving the way for fear to grow. This dynamic sheds light on why many spiritual traditions link fear closely with the ego—an intricate relationship we'll delve into later in this book.

Up to this point, we've explored how childhood experiences lay the foundation for the inner voices that shape our thoughts and emotions. As fear infiltrates these inner narratives, it magnifies feelings of insecurity, isolation, and anxiety, creating a mental landscape dominated by unease.

To truly unlock greater mental wellbeing, it's helpful to explore the spiritual concepts of duality and non-duality, as taught by ancient traditions. These teachings reveal how judgments—whether directed at ourselves or others—fuel fear and reinforce separation. By shifting from duality to non-duality, we dismantle the barriers of judgment and division, unlocking more profound peace and mental clarity. This shift opens the path to greater wellbeing, allowing us to step beyond the fear-based stories that keep us trapped in cycles of inner conflict.

Duality and the Invisible Boundary Lines

Our physical world is inherently dualistic: up or down, north or south, left or right, night or day, light or darkness. These fundamental dichotomies enable us to describe and navigate our perception of reality. They allow us to distinguish between light and dark, male and female, offering a schema for understanding our environment. The absence of darkness in space would render the stars' light invisible. Masculinity would be intangible without femininity, and vice versa. These contrasts enrich our lives, providing clarity and depth to our perception of the world.

However, such dualities also harbor a less beneficial side, particularly when judgments intertwine with these binary distinctions. Consider the dualities of believer versus non-believer, gay versus straight, Christian versus Muslim, American versus Chinese, black versus white. These labels do serve practical purposes in our everyday lives by helping us distinguish between different concepts. However, we often align these categories on a spectrum that reflects our unconscious biases, interpreting one side as "good" and the other as "bad."

When judgment enters the equation, it manifests as an inner critical voice that condemns. This voice draws lines in the sand, categorizing one side as positive and the other as unfavorable. Invariably, we position ourselves on the "right" side of these divides, viewing our side of the boundary line as just and virtuous, while anything on the opposite side is perceived, at the very least, as less virtuous, if not outright wrong.

The story of Adam and Eve in the Garden of Eden vividly exemplifies how these boundary lines penetrate human consciousness, leading to fear and a wide range of negative emotions. Esoteric Jewish interpretations of the biblical story suggest that Adam and Eve first existed in a higher dimension of consciousness. They perceived the world as unified, embodying a profound connection that transcended physical distinctions.

In the story, Adam's and Eve's physical nakedness symbolized more than just their lack of clothing. It also represented complete transparency, where nothing was hidden, neither external nor internal. Their lives resembled an open book, devoid of any secrets from each other and the world around them. In this state of consciousness, Adam and Eve experienced no shame, despite being naked. They existed in unity with one another and God. This unity consciousness made their physical distinctions irrelevant. They did not identify with their bodies, but rather with the divine essence of life breathed into them. In this harmonious state, there was no room for shame or fear.

However, the serpent's suggestion that they eat from the fruit of the Tree of Knowledge of Good and Evil introduced a profound shift. Think of the trees in this story as mental frameworks through which we understand and navigate our existence, with the Tree of Knowledge representing a dualistic way of interpreting reality. Jesus likened these conceptual frameworks to wineskins, reflecting his era's cultural and temporal context. In today's terms, these frameworks function much like a computer's operating system. Just as an operating system determines how a computer processes information, interacts with users, and executes tasks, these mental frameworks shape how we process experiences, form self-perceptions, and interpret the world around us. They are the unseen structures that govern the way we "operate" in life.

To unpack this, let's first examine the nature of *knowledge* portrayed in this story. Knowledge encompasses all the information we have accumulated in our memory from past experiences—events we've encountered, subjects we've studied, and personal experiences. It is intrinsically bound to the dimension of time, being dependent on past information. Without time, memory would not exist, rendering the knowledge discussed in this story nonexistent.

Contrastingly, *knowing* or being *aware* is fundamentally different from possessing knowledge. This distinction is elegantly articulated in the biblical narrative, where Paul writes, "that you may *know* (ginōskō) the love of Christ which surpasses *knowledge* (gnōsis)."[3] Here, Paul distinguishes between *knowing* and *knowledge*, suggesting that we can be aware of something beyond the confines of acquired knowledge. While knowledge is a construct of the mind, a collection of memories and learned information, knowing is about being fully present in the timeless now.

Consider the experience of watching whales breaching off the coast. In that moment, you're acutely aware of their powerful movements. This awareness doesn't depend on labeling the experience, recalling its scientific basis, or retrieving past memories of similar events. You are simply there, fully present, immersed in the experience. Yet, when you reflect on those whales, days or years later, you engage with knowledge. You remember standing there, witnessing the whales emerge from the water. This scenario captures the essence of the distinction between knowing and knowledge: The former is about being present and directly aware, while the latter involves engaging with information and memories from the past.

Thus, the Tree of Knowledge of Good and Evil represents a way of understanding and experiencing reality grounded in past experiences. It doesn't matter when these experiences happened—five seconds or several years ago. Once they're in the past, the exact amount of time doesn't matter.

But this tree doesn't just cover all knowledge from our past. It focuses on how we *judge* past events as good or bad, right or wrong, based on how they made us feel. We reflect on what occurred and then form an emotionally charged judgment about that particular event. For instance, if someone's behavior toward you was kind, you may consider their actions good, encoding this judgment in your memory. On the other hand, if their actions brought about sorrow or resentment, you would likely categorize these actions as bad or evil.

When you judge a past experience, whether it's about someone else's actions, your own behavior, or any other detail of that experience, you're essentially drawing an invisible or illusionary boundary line in your mind. This boundary line delineates between what is considered good and not good enough, separating perceived positive elements from negative ones.

The issue with drawing such a line is that the boundary line becomes the root of conflict. Our judgments form a mental boundary, separating our sense of self from what we label "bad." Our judgments cover a broad spectrum, setting up invisible boundary lines in our minds that cultivate a sense of separation. Such boundary lines become an internal battlefield, leading to a struggle that causes suffering and disrupts our inner peace. Every experience that carries emotional weight for us becomes one of these mental barriers.

Take relationships as an example. We often unconsciously compare ourselves to others, leading to feelings of either being lesser or better than them. In many close relationships, these comparisons find a balance. We might feel superior in some ways but inferior in others, creating a balance that fosters strong friendships. These judgments usually don't carry heavy emotions, which helps make the friendship last.

But, when feelings of being lesser or greater are strong and unbalanced, they block the development of deep connections. Feeling constantly inferior to someone can cause us to pull away from them. On the flip side, thinking we're far superior can make us avoid others, fearing their shortcomings might tarnish our image. When we engage in acts of kindness toward those we see as beneath us, it's often not in pursuit of a relationship but rather to alleviate our guilt and bolster our self-image, or because we want something from them.

What this means is that we draw mental boundary lines that distinguish us from others, crafting an illusion of difference and opposition. This isn't just about personal relationships but also affects broader social divides like race, gender, sexual orientation, nationality, religion, and politics. These judgments create biases, both conscious and unconscious, forming invisible barriers that often cast others as on the "bad" side while we see ourselves as on the "good" side.

On a personal level, the judgments we cast upon ourselves, especially concerning our mistakes, erode our sense of self. We draw a boundary line around the aspects of ourselves we deem failures, trying to conceal or escape them. Yet, these aspects are merely suppressed in our unconscious memory, evolving into a feeling of being less than enough. This suppression doesn't eliminate the underlying emotions but instead converts them into a source of shame that shapes our personality and steers our actions, behaviors, and interactions with others.

When we face reminders of these hidden parts, it puts pressure on this internal boundary, sparking fear and leading to responses like anger, anxiety, withdrawing into depression, or adopting a victim mentality.

For instance, consider someone who once felt they failed at public speaking. The embarrassment and judgment they placed on themselves for this failure might lead them to avoid speaking situations, fearing a repeat of past shame. This avoidance becomes a boundary, a limit they dare not cross, rooted in the knowledge of being "less than" others in their own eyes.

However, when a job promotion requires them to make a presentation in front of an audience, that invisible boundary is pressured, surfacing fear and triggering a disproportionate response—anger at the situation, deep anxiety, withdrawal from the opportunity, and/or a resigned belief that they are simply not good enough, embodying the victim stance. Such responses only reinforce the boundary line and the belief in their inadequacy, illustrating how deeply internal judgments influence our life choices and wellbeing.

Judging our actions as superior can also pave the way for suffering. When we perceive ourselves as having done something commendable, we demarcate the achievement and embed it within our subconscious. It then becomes entwined with our self-perception—our personality or egoic identity. If someone fails to recognize this positive aspect, downplays it, or outright dismisses it, resentment can grow. This resentment, a form of judgment, also establishes a mental boundary line. Such feelings of bitterness become a source of suffering, potentially sparking both inner stress and conflicts with other people.

A Father's Story of Overcoming Resentment

Once, after I delivered a talk at a conference in London, a gentleman approached me as the crowd began to dissipate from the auditorium. He introduced himself as John, and we found ourselves seated in the front row, enveloped in the quiet aftermath of the event. John shared with me that he had attended one of my seminars a couple of years earlier, which had profoundly impacted his relationship with his daughter, Jenny.

He explained how, after Jenny had grown up, he was frequently upset and angry with her—a puzzling sensation, since he deeply loved his daughter and had always been her pillar. He reminisced about Jenny's childhood, a time filled with father-daughter trips around the globe and his constant encouragement for her to chase her dreams. John's narrative then took a turn as he spoke of Jenny's mother, a woman who had struggled with severe depression during Jenny's early years. To protect Jenny, John would take her along on business trips, shielding her from her mother's turmoil.

However, as Jenny transitioned into adulthood, her mother amazingly overcame most of her struggles, finding freedom from past wounds. John, who had once divorced Jenny's mother, chose to remarry her. In this new chapter, Jenny developed a strong bond with her mother, gravitating toward her and spending significant time together—leaving John feeling sidelined.

John's voice softened as he confessed that he had drawn a mental boundary line around his good parenting, constantly comparing himself to his wife and casting himself as the superior parent. Witnessing Jenny's growing closeness with her mother stirred resentment within him. He felt that his love and the efforts he poured into raising Jenny had been forgotten or overlooked. Whenever he was with Jenny, irritation and judgment clouded his interactions. Unbeknownst to him, jealousy had taken root, overshadowed by a sense that he deserved more recognition.

Driven by the insights gained from the seminar, John dedicated the following three weeks to cultivating an atmosphere of grace through meditation. He embraced the present moment, allowing peace and unconditional love to permeate his being. In this space of inner stillness, he bravely revisited his feelings of resentment, allowing them to surface and acknowledging them with compassion and forgiveness. Remarkably, this process led to the dissolution of the negative feelings he harbored toward his daughter, and the critical inner voices that had been driving his anger. Since that transformative period, John shared, there had been no arguments, anger, or resentment. He expressed genuine joy for the flourishing relationship between Jenny and her mother, a sentiment that once seemed unattainable.

John's story vividly illustrates how the internal boundaries we erect can obscure the beauty of our relationships. It also highlights the healing that can unfold when we confront these mental divisions with unconditional love, guiding us toward reconciliation and genuine contentment.

So when we're tempted to believe that a better future is out of reach, we can take comfort in knowing that the chaos within the mind doesn't have to be permanent. Instead, it serves as an invitation to look deeper, gain understanding, and awaken to the inner stillness and unconditional love that lie at the core of our being. It's the same journey Matthew embarked on, searching for answers to the destructive chatter in his head and ultimately finding an inner peace that surpasses all understanding—proof that transformation is possible and within reach.

3

RESHAPING OUR REALITY

One day, I received a message from Barbara, who felt her life was in a relentless downward spiral. Health issues had rendered her unable to maintain steady employment. To compound her challenges, her savings were depleted, and amidst these adversities, her husband of twenty-five years decided to leave. Overwhelmed with guilt, she blamed herself for her husband's departure. Rather than pursuing financial support or considering a divorce that could provide her with some financial security, she clung to the current state of things, holding onto a faint glimmer of hope that circumstances might shift.

But as days turned into weeks, she lost her grip on hope. Many nights, Barbara prayed for an end, for life to be over. Her pleas were born from a cocoon of despair that enveloped her, blocking any semblance of light or hope.

Barbara's family tried to penetrate this cocoon, assuring her of new beginnings and promising support. But their words seemed to bounce off an impenetrable barrier. No affirmation or assurance could reshape the reality she was trapped in.

After engaging in several conversations with Barbara, I introduced her to a transformational program: a forty-day discovery course with teachings and meditations, designed to foster a spirituality rooted in inner peace and unconditional love. Initially, Barbara approached meditation with hesitation, finding the practice unfamiliar. However, as she immersed herself in the program, she experienced a profound shift in her emotional landscape. Her anxiety began to wane, giving way to a serenity that soared beyond her external challenges. This newfound peace was coupled with a deep, unconditional love that surged from within, independent of her circumstances.

Barbara didn't just go through the program once. Rather, it became integral to her ongoing routine. Every time Barbara went through the program, her life got a little brighter. It was like watching someone turn on the lights in a room that had been dark for too long. She started seeing things differently, with a wisdom that arose from deep within, making her daily battles much less daunting. This wasn't just about getting by anymore. It was a complete overhaul of her inner world. And as her inner reality transformed, her outer world started to change too. She got out of debt, made great friends, and even landed her dream job. This wasn't just luck. Barbara had awakened to an inner peace—a heightened awareness of her true self, and that shift inside her had turned her world around.

Barbara's story is a powerful reminder that real change starts within. I'm not saying everything becomes perfect overnight, or you'll suddenly hit the jackpot and all your problems disappear. But undoubtedly, we cannot come to any other conclusion than that a shift in our inner world transforms our outer reality.

Around the globe, I've encountered countless individuals who, much like Barbara initially did, feel stuck, weighed down by their past, and unable to see a way out of their current mess. They're like birds in a cage, seeing bits of the sky but unable to reach it, trapped in a cocoon made not of silk, but of their own fears and painful memories. It's tough to imagine a different life when you're wrapped up in that kind of darkness.

Such darkness can be likened to standing in a room lined with mirrors, each reflecting back our insecurities, failures, and the echoing voice that whispers, "You are not enough." These reflections distort our perception, turning the room into a maze where every turn leads to another dead end. The repeated image of our perceived inadequacies intensifies the weight of our current struggles, making the idea of a brighter tomorrow seem like a far-fetched dream.

It's not just the circumstance itself that's stifling. There's the amalgamation of every setback we've faced, every *no* we've heard, and every time we've felt less than enough. This conditioning has led us to believe that these mirrors show the only reality and that any other narrative is a mere illusion.

Yet, if we take anything from stories like Barbara's, it's that our toughest times serve as catalysts for shedding outdated patterns and perceptions. We often become ready to break free through our desperation and the challenges that seem impossible to overcome. Thus, feeling trapped like a caterpillar stuck in a cocoon is the beginning of a profound transformation. It's tough to see it when we are right in the middle of it all, but those struggles might just be getting us ready to break free and soar, like a butterfly finally spreading its wings.

The Interplay Between Reality and Our Perception of It

Understanding the intricate relationship between reality and our perception of it is crucial for reframing and transforming our reality. This dynamic raises an important question: Does reality mold our perception, or does our perception construct our reality?

Our circumstances, especially those we are born into, often appear as preset stages upon which our lives play out. For instance, someone born in a modest hut in an impoverished village in Africa had no influence over their birthplace. Their mindset or feelings didn't choose that reality. Similarly, consider a child growing up in a crime-ridden, densely populated urban environment with limited access to quality education. Their childhood and day-to-day existence under the shadow of violence aren't a product of their thoughts or emotions.

Yet, it's equally true that our feelings, attitudes, and perspectives hold considerable sway over how we experience life and create our reality. Our reactions to events, our resilience in the face of challenges, and our ability to find hope or despair in situations are all shaped by our internal beliefs and feelings.

Take, for example, the case of Barbara. Some aspects of her life were undeniably out of her control. We can't dictate how every facet of our lives will pan out. However, other parts of her experience were shaped by her perceptions and how she chose to engage with her reality.

This dynamic interplay suggests that while objective reality exists—containing immutable events and circumstances beyond our control—our subjective reality, the world as we experience it, is deeply colored by our perceptions. Understanding this can empower us to alter our perspective and, in turn, influence our lived experience, even if we can't always immediately change the external events themselves. Yet, by grasping the principles that determine the reality we experience, we can begin right now to create a new future. We can reshape our circumstances and chart a new course in life.

What Is Reality?

Humans have a curious relationship with reality. We are constantly immersed in it, yet defining or fully comprehending it eludes us. It appears robust and tangible, yet on closer inspection, it dissipates like a mirage. Its origin, scale, trajectory, and purpose remain mysterious to us.

Yet, if we attempt to decipher reality, we might say it embraces everything in existence. This includes the vastness of space, the palpable substance of matter, and the elusive forces of energy. It also covers the domain of consciousness and the activities of our minds—our thoughts and emotions—that give us the capacity to perceive and interpret our surroundings.

At first glance, reality can be partitioned into three distinct categories, often labeled as objective, subjective, and intersubjective reality. Objective reality refers to the reality that exists independently of our perception or interpretation of that reality. For example, the fact that the Earth revolves around the sun is an objective reality.

Subjective reality, on the other hand, refers to reality based on our personal perceptions, beliefs, and interpretations. It is subjective because it can vary from person to person. For example, two people can look at the same painting and have entirely different interpretations of its meaning. One might see a depiction of tranquility and peace, while the other perceives it as a representation of loneliness and isolation, influenced by their personal experiences and emotions.

Intersubjective reality refers to the reality shared by a group of individuals with a common understanding or agreement. This reality is created through social interaction and communication between people. For instance, money as a valuable resource is an example of intersubjective reality. While paper money has no inherent value, our collective belief in its worth and acceptance as a medium of exchange gives it power and significance.

Navigating further into the nature of reality, we encounter the question of a reality that exists beyond our perception and personal experiences. The notion of a reality extending beyond our awareness might invite skepticism. However, the absence of our awareness doesn't equate to nonexistence. It simply means we're not conscious of it.

Quantum physics theory suggests that all things are interconnected. We are part of a larger system of particles constantly interacting and exchanging energy and information, suggesting a transcending reality beyond what we can observe. It's happening in and through us yet transcending all things. However, despite its existence, we are unaware of it. It is real, but it remains unreal to us since we have not experienced it through our sense perception.

This concept of a hidden, interconnected reality may not be very satisfying unless you enjoy exploring the world of "quantum weirdness." The challenge is that unless we experience something for ourselves, it does not seem real to us. But is something untrue just because we personally have not experienced it? Of course not. Most of us have no problem believing what we have been taught, even though we may not have personally experienced it. For example, many people believe in the existence of historical events, like the signing of the Declaration of Independence, even though they did not witness it themselves, trusting the accounts of historians and the evidence left behind.

Yet we know from studies that our brains develop cognitive biases and heuristics, based on our past experiences, that help us make sense of the world. These biases can cause us to reject new information that does not fit within our existing mental models and experiences. So, when we contemplate a reality beyond what we have observed or experienced, our natural skepticism and reluctance to accept new information can prevent us from exploring these mysteries fully. We may even reject the ideas and experiences of others that don't fit within our worldview.

Barbara's story exemplifies this cognitive bias. She struggled to entertain the possibility of a life different from what she'd known. Her perspective was tightly bound to a preconceived notion of how her life should unfold. In the grips of depression, it's challenging to envision an alternative reality. Barbara's upbringing, with a view of a God ready to punish any disobedience, compounded her predicament, making her prone to feelings of guilt and shame, which led her to self-blame. Furthermore, her religious teachings had imbued her with the ideal of a flawless marriage, leaving her initially in denial when faced with the stark reality that her marriage might be over.

She believed that acquiring money would be the solution to wooing her husband back into her life. Barbara clung to the idea of her husband's return, as that was the sole reality that brought her a semblance of security. Even in the face of his departure, she strategized her actions, hoping to lure him back. However, the rift between them only widened.

The answer was to help her reframe her feelings about her present situation. Barbara needed to reach a state of acceptance of *what is* and gratitude for her life. This would enable her to envision and embrace a new reality vastly different from her long-held beliefs and worldview.

The dark cloud that hovered over Barbara's mind had to dissipate. Only when the light of consciousness shines brightly with love would she be able to see the limitless possibilities available to her. This approach aligns with a fundamental principle of quantum physics, which suggests that consciousness plays a significant role in shaping our reality. When our consciousness is clear and unobstructed by our conditioned mind, the realm of possibilities we can explore and embrace becomes boundless.

Changing Your Reality: Insights from the Intriguing Quantum Realm

In the Newtonian model of physics, all matter was considered solid. This mechanistic view influenced thinking for centuries, leading many to perceive humans as mere subjects of circumstances with little sway over reality. However, the advent of quantum physics challenged this static worldview.

Niels Bohr, Max Planck, Albert Einstein, and their contemporaries unveiled findings so unconventional that they initially seemed implausible. While the extensive world of matter behaved predictably, the microscopic realm of atoms and subatomic particles didn't conform to established physical laws.

These particles, the fundamental building blocks of existence, exhibited peculiar behaviors. They momentarily manifested in the realm of time, space, and matter, only to vanish into an undefined quantum field—apart from time, space, and matter.

Where did they go? They transitioned into what physicists call quantum waves or states of potentiality. These waves have measurable frequencies but do not have a fixed space position. They transcend matter. They are not material but rather trans-material.

Think of them less as solid entities and more akin to thought-like patterns. They exist in a state of "nowhere." Yet, they can emerge out of their state of potentiality when observed or measured, causing what physicists call a "collapse of the wave function." This phenomenon is referred to as the "observer effect," where the act of observation itself influences the state of the observed particles.

This discovery illustrates how a conscious observation or interaction can manifest a formless quantum wave of information into tangible entities within our three-dimensional world. It raises compelling questions about the role of consciousness in manifesting reality. If the act of observation can "collapse" a wave function into a tangible entity, then theoretically, isn't it possible that our conscious observation might influence the physical world more than we previously imagined?

Then there's this fascinating concept that physicists call "quantum entanglement." When two particles become entangled, their properties become interlinked, no matter the distance between them. This means that the state of one particle is immediately connected to the state of the other, regardless of how far apart they are.

For example, imagine two entangled particles, each spinning in an uncertain direction. In the moment that we measure one particle and find it spinning in a particular direction, let's say up, the entangled partner would instantaneously be found to spin in the down direction. This occurs even if the two particles are light-years apart, demonstrating a non-local connection that transcends the bounds of classical physics.

Albert Einstein famously referred to quantum entanglement as "spooky action at a distance" because it challenges our intuitive understanding of the world. On one hand, it suggests that information can travel faster than light. On the other hand, it contradicts Einstein's theory of relativity, which doesn't allow for faster-than-light communication or information transfer. So, what does this mean? It suggests a profound underlying connectedness in the universe that is fundamentally different from our everyday experience of reality.

Considering both "the observer effect" and "quantum entanglement" suggests a profound relationship between consciousness and physical reality. The observer effect posits that simply observing or measuring a system changes its state. Meanwhile, quantum entanglement reveals that particles can become so deeply connected that the state of one instantly influences the other, regardless of the distance between them.

These phenomena point to a deep, intrinsic interconnectedness in reality, suggesting that our individual consciousness may influence or even cocreate the reality we experience. Far from being passive observers, we are active participants in a grand, cosmic tapestry, bound together by the threads of consciousness.

To deepen this perspective, consider the idea that God is the ultimate consciousness, and we are each an expression of that consciousness, much like light rays emanating from the sun. While the rays are not the sun, they are inseparable from it. Similarly, we are not God, but the essence of God, as the ultimate consciousness, flows through us. Our personal consciousness, then, is not an isolated entity but an emanation from and interconnection with the One-Life and ultimate consciousness. In this way, we are cocreators with God, sharing in the act of shaping reality.

When we focus on observing a specific element, we can reframe and even create a new reality. Essentially, our awareness, attention, and intention play pivotal roles in reshaping our experiences. We can bring about new outcomes by aligning our thoughts and feelings with our desired goals.

Four States of Wakeful Consciousness

Our exploration thus far shows that we play an active role in creating our reality. We've recognized that the intangible elements of our thoughts, emotions, imaginations, and state of consciousness heavily influence the reality we manifest. Does our experience emanate from a profound inner calm, or is it overshadowed by fear? Are we navigating our reality from a peaceful state or one filled with stress and anxiety?

How we feel on the inside deeply colors our perception of the world outside, and this perception, in turn, molds our lived experience. Over time, the nature of our experiences, woven together daily, crafts the fabric of the reality we come to inhabit.

Throughout the course of the day, our interior feeling state tends to oscillate, influenced by our bodily condition and the focal point of our thoughts.[1] The most natural state of wakeful consciousness is characterized by "calm." This is the juncture where our intellectual capacity is optimized, enabling creativity and logic to thrive, thus leading to wisdom and problem-solving. This state also fosters increased compassion and kindness toward our fellow human beings and all creation.

Following calm, we encounter the "alert" state, marked by an external focus—whether it be a task at work or home or engaging in a conversation, concentrating on speaking or listening. Both calm and alert states are pivotal for an optimal human experience.

However, events during the day can disrupt this balance, thrusting us into an "alarm" state triggered by feelings of threat, challenge, surprise, or attack. Emotions amplify during this state, whereas intelligence, logic, creativity, and even love for others dwindle. This state can often result in regrettable actions or arguments with family, friends, colleagues, and sometimes strangers.

The alarm state can intensify to a "fear" state if the perceived threat becomes overwhelming. In this state, self-preservation takes precedence, and our internal response mechanism prepares us for fight, flight, or freeze. Consequently, our cognitive and problem-solving abilities deteriorate. At its extreme, fear can escalate to "terror," where emotional control is lost, possibly resulting in violence. Logic, creativity, and feelings of love and compassion disappear entirely.

The real issue arises when a person gets trapped in a continuous state of alert, alarm, and/or fear. For instance, someone constantly on alert might struggle with forgetfulness, lose belongings, daydream excessively, talk too much, or have trouble resisting temptations, making them prone to unnecessary risks.

Alternatively, individuals trapped in the alarm state tend to resist change, circumstances, and people. They often display defiance toward authority figures. A child in such a state might act out against their parents or refuse to comply with a new school scenario, leading to disruptive behavior. Adults may question decisions, resist following instructions, or become confrontational at work or other institutions like health clinics or government agencies.

When people are stuck in a state of fear, they tend to avoid or escape the source of that fear. A child being bullied at school, if constantly nagged by parents about the issue, might avoid their parents and continuously seek ways to escape the threatening school environment.

And when individuals are in an acute state of fear or terror, they might feel the only way to regain control or momentarily alleviate their inner pain is to retaliate. They may get outraged and even verbally abusive. In extreme cases, they may resort to aggressive behavior and violence, impacting their familial relationships and careers and even leading to criminal activity, including imprisonment or death.

Thus, it's evident that our inner subjective state steers how we perceive life. This perception molds our reality, and, in turn, this shaped reality influences our future experiences. Consequently, everything from our health to our relationships and even our pursuits in life are significantly influenced by our internal subjective state.

Recognizing this pattern and acknowledging our inner state's profound influence on shaping our experiences equip us with the potential for transformation. Questions then arise:

How can we transform our perception of reality to foster improved health, enriched relationships, and a purpose-filled life?

What steps are necessary to shatter entrenched inner patterns of stress, anxiety, guilt, shame, and other emotions and supplant them with a state of inner wholeness?

Transcending Pain—Consciousness, Love, and a New Reality

As indicated earlier, I was raised in the Christian faith and had the opportunity to lead several wonderful congregations as a pastor in both Canada and California. I was even privileged to travel the globe, speaking at conferences, churches, and festivals, sometimes to crowds of 10,000 to 75,000 people.

Despite these opportunities, however, I grappled with a torrent of toxic emotions, such as guilt, anger, and anxiety. My interpretation of truth was not providing the relief I sought. The harder I tried, the more acutely I felt the nagging sensation that something was missing, that I was somehow not enough, and that I was failing to live up to the expectations of God, myself, and others.

My struggle reached a crescendo in 2005 when I developed a condition known as cluster headaches. This uncommon headache disorder is infamous for its intense and debilitating pain. Named "cluster" due to the cyclical nature of its attacks, the pain is often described as sharp, burning, or piercing, usually localized on one side of the head. The onset is abrupt, and the peak pain intense. It left me feeling like a knife was twisting in my eye.

The pain was excruciating, lasting anywhere from fifteen minutes to three hours, and it would strike multiple times a day. The exact physical cause of cluster headaches remains unclear, but they're believed to be connected to the sudden release of histamine or serotonin in the brain.

These substances significantly influence our brain functions and emotional state, regulating sleep-wake cycles, mood, and stress responses. Disruptions in the levels or activities of histamine or serotonin can contribute to various health problems, including cluster headaches. In my case, it would seem as if the deep emotional states of guilt and anxiety had triggered these cluster headaches.

During this period, I felt enveloped by a sense of hopelessness, teetering on the brink of surrender. But then, following a ferocious bout of cluster headaches one night in 2006, I felt an urge to meditate. As a novice, I chose my car as my sanctuary.

With Jesus symbolizing pure love to me, I directed my focus toward a specific scene from Mel Gibson's movie *The Passion of the Christ*, a depiction that resonated deeply with me. I was flooded with an overwhelming sense of love as I immersed myself in this image.

This love transcended empirical reality. It was beyond the realm of the physical or the material. As I shifted my attention toward this pure love, the pain subsided. It felt like the cluttered debris of my *soul*, burdened with guilt, anger, and fear, suddenly cleared, allowing the unobstructed flow of love from infinite consciousness into my individual consciousness.

This inner awareness of unity facilitated the manifestation of physical wholeness, a new reality. My lens of perception shifted from fear to love, causing the wave of physical wholeness to collapse into tangible reality.

My experience is my own, yet it illustrates a universal lesson that extends to every corner of the human experience. From the expanses of the cosmos to the enigmatic dance of subatomic particles to the throbbing pain of a cluster headache, we've witnessed the fascinating connection between consciousness and reality.

One fact is certain: We each have the power to shift our reality. This power doesn't lie in a mysterious incantation or an elusive secret—it rests within our consciousness.

Experiencing a holistic reality doesn't necessitate a drastic outward change. Instead, the inner transformation, the shift from fear to love, the terrestrial to the transcending, paves the way for a new, more harmonious outer reality to emerge.

Your reality directly reflects your perception, shaped and molded by your beliefs, emotions, and past experiences. Cultivating inner wholeness allows you to reconfigure this perception, adjusting the filter through which you perceive your world.

As this filter changes, your reality follows suit. When your *soul* liberates itself from the chains of fear and opens to the boundless, unifying love at the heart of existence, the reality you experience begins to align with this elevated frequency.

What untapped opportunities are waiting for you to discover? Can you replace the fear-warped lens through which you may have viewed reality? What new reality might you now observe once this lens is replaced with a state of inner stillness? As we continue to focus on that inner dimension, metaphorically referred to as the ascending life, the answers to these questions will emerge, providing a pathway to a transformative shift in our perception and, consequently, our reality.

The next step in this transformational journey is understanding who you truly are. Only by knowing your true self—through an inner awareness—can you perceive and experience reality from an ascending place. This understanding also unlocks the potential to manifest a new reality, one that's founded on the boundless potential resting within the depths of your existence.

4

KNOW THYSELF

When you look in the mirror, you see a reflection —an image shaped by time, experiences, and life's many adventures. You might notice the laugh lines etched by countless smiles, the battle scars from old wounds, and the physical marks that tell a story unique to you. We often attribute our identity to these physical features, believing that who we are is defined by what we see.

Beyond the physical, we also weave together memories, societal roles, and personal beliefs into a self-image. This patchwork becomes our personality—a blend of traits, interests, values, abilities, and emotions. It's the narrative we create about who we are, pieced together from our successes, failures, roles, and belief systems.

Yet, we limit ourselves when we define ourselves primarily by our personality. If we think the story we've crafted is the entirety of who we are, we tie our self-worth to external validation—whether through success, approval or how well we fit into societal norms. But because the external world constantly changes, any identity based on it becomes fragile. This leads to inner turmoil, as we find ourselves reacting to every setback, criticism, or perceived flaw, reinforcing feelings of inadequacy.

Holding tightly to this identity also gives us a false sense of separation. The more we cling to a fixed idea of who we are, the more we judge and compare ourselves to others. We either feel superior or diminish ourselves by feeling less than others. This constant comparison keeps us in a cycle of dissatisfaction, blocking us from recognizing the deeper unity that connects us all. Our personality becomes a prison, keeping us from experiencing the boundless awareness that lies beneath.

By identifying with our personality, we perpetuate the illusion that we are our thoughts, beliefs, and emotions rather than recognizing that we are the awareness in which these experiences arise. This misidentification results in inner conflict, anxiety, and a sense of incompleteness. We seek fulfillment in the outside world—through achievements, possessions, or relationships—believing these will complete our story. But these pursuits often leave us feeling even more disconnected, as true peace and wholeness can only be found when we are aware of the deeper consciousness that transcends the narrative of our personality.

To move beyond this self-imposed limitation, we must shift our awareness away from the personality and awaken to the ever-present essence within us. This is the space of inner stillness, where we are not defined by our past or limited by our beliefs. Here, we discover that our true nature is one of peace, love, and unity—a boundless reality free from suffering. This awakening allows us to live authentically, no longer controlled by the stories we tell ourselves but guided by the deep, transcendent wisdom and expansive awareness that flows from our innermost being.

This can feel abstract and difficult to grasp, especially when we are deeply identified with our personality, as most of humanity is. So, in this chapter, I want to make a clear case for who we are beyond personality. While the personality has value, true mental wellbeing is rooted in a deeper awareness of our true essence. Awakening to this essence forms the foundation for lasting inner peace and fulfillment.

To explore this awakening, we must first ask: where, within ourselves, do we truly uncover our deepest essence? This question invites us to look beyond the surface layers of our self-constructed identity—those shaped by roles, beliefs, and experiences—and shift our focus inward.

Where in You are YOU?

We often ask ourselves, "Who am I?"—a question that revolves around our personality and our roles in life. While this is an interesting question, and plenty of research and personality tests are exploring it, a more accurate question for unlocking greater mental wellbeing begins with, "What am I?" Understanding the essence of what we truly are is the foundation for creating a boundless reality rooted in inner wholeness and transcendence.

So, what are you? At first glance, you are a body—somewhat gory on the inside, yet beautiful on the outside. Science offers us a plethora of intriguing facts about the human body. For starters, it contains approximately 60 percent water. Most of that water resides within the cells, vital for their survival.

Speaking of cells, the body comprises around 75 trillion of them. Each cell houses hundreds of thousands of molecules, with six feet of DNA in every cell encoding three billion genetic instructions. Documenting these codes for just one of our 75 trillion cells would necessitate 1,000 books, each around 600 pages long.

A closer examination of one cell reveals the presence of approximately 75 trillion atoms, indicative of their incredibly minute size. More fascinating yet, these atoms are 99.9 percent empty space—an invisible energy field. Atoms are the basic units of chemical elements. They bond with other atoms, creating a perpetual, frenetic swirl of activity. This movement of energy morphs into cells, which join together to form patterns that constitute heart, bones, hair, and teeth, as well as personality, habits, and memories.

Interestingly, atoms aren't stationary. The atoms that constitute you at this moment could have formerly been a part of Mars or Bruno Mars, Jesus or Buddha, an extraterrestrial being (if they exist), or your neighborhood cat. While the pattern stays mostly constant, the atoms move in unpredictable directions and velocities.

Another less pleasant fact is that we all shed hundreds of hair strands daily. Therefore, don't be alarmed if you spot some of your hair on your pillow in the morning. As for the source of the dust in your home, your skin is the primary contributor, constituting 90 percent of your household dust. You shed around ten billion skin flakes daily, resulting in your skin undergoing a complete rejuvenation every twenty-eight days. Approximately every seven to nine years, your entire body goes through a total cellular renewal.

Yet, throughout all these changes, "you" continue to be YOU. This prompts the question: Where are you within the embodied form? To amplify the conundrum, consider this: When you were a five-year-old child, weren't you experiencing what it felt like to be five? Later, at fifteen, when you saw a fifteen-year-old figure in the mirror, wasn't it you acknowledging the transformation? And now, doesn't that same "you" observe the changes that time has inscribed on your body and mind?

The constant throughout these instances isn't the physical body that changes with time, nor your evolving thoughts and emotions about yourself. Instead, it is the persistent awareness of being "you."

This begs the question: Where are you located within your body? You are aware of your existence, but where does this awareness originate, and where does it reside?

Science, thus far, fails to provide adequate answers to such questions. As Dr. Robert Lanza suggests:

> *Nothing in modern physics explains how a group of molecules in your brain create consciousness.... Nothing in science can explain how consciousness arose from matter.... The beauty of a sunset, the miracle of falling in love, the taste of a delicious meal—these are all mysteries to modern science.*[1]

Despite our immense knowledge, consciousness remains a scientific enigma. Dr. Lanza further postulates that "without consciousness, 'matter' dwells in an undetermined state of probability. Any universe that could have preceded consciousness only existed in a probability state."[2]

This idea aligns with discussions from the previous chapter, which suggested that particles appear to behave differently when observed, a phenomenon known as the "observer effect." This concept hints at a deep connection between consciousness and the fabric of the universe. It's a fascinating notion, suggesting that our perceptions and awareness not only shape our reality but also blur the distinctions between the tangible and intangible— between matter and energy or the physical and the spiritual.

From this, we can conclude that even though our cells are constantly regenerating and atoms are always in flux, something deeper endures. A continuous presence or consciousness remains—a force that breathes life into the body we live in, anchoring us in a reality that goes beyond the ever-shifting physical world.

What Is Consciousness?

Consciousness, at its essence, is simply our awareness—of ourselves and the world around us. It is the quiet observer within, the presence that witnesses our thoughts, feels our emotions, and perceives our sensations. In its simplest form, consciousness is the inner space where all experiences unfold. It is not the experience itself but the formless presence in which every experience arises. Without this awareness, there would be no perceptions, thoughts, emotions, or dreams. This formless presence is the truest essence of who we are.

One common metaphor for consciousness is light, symbolizing an illuminating force that unveils reality and fosters life. First, let's contemplate the profound link between light and life. Light is the lifeblood of existence as we understand it. Plants seize the energy of light through photosynthesis to generate nourishment, while animals depend on it to modulate biological processes and synchronize their internal biological clocks. Light and life are profoundly interwoven in this elaborate ballet of existence, each incapable of existing without the other.

Secondly, light serves as a metaphor for the entity that reveals reality. When Jesus declared, "You are the light of the world," he essentially said, "You are consciousness." Without consciousness, there can be no experience of the world. In this context, consciousness is a radiant beacon that lights our existence. It's our true self—the cornerstone for the ascending life.

The Timeless "I Am"

In our spiritual texts, one of the clearest examples of consciousness can be found in the Book of Exodus, when God reveals Godself to Moses as "I Am that I Am." This phrase communicates more than a name; it conveys a state of pure being, an existence beyond physical form, time, or space. It represents an awareness that simply *is*—unchanging, formless, and timeless. In other words, this "I Am" can be understood as a declaration of pure consciousness.

Why is "I Am" synonymous with consciousness? Let's break it down. At its core, consciousness is the awareness of existence—the recognition that *I am*. Before anything else can be known or experienced, we must be conscious. The phrase "I Am" captures this foundational awareness. It is not tied to identity, roles, or external conditions but refers to the simple awareness of existence, which is the essence of consciousness.

In Jewish tradition, when God breathes into man's nostrils the breath of life, it is a metaphor for consciousness being embedded into the individual. This breath (spirit or *ruach* in Hebrew) makes humans aware beings, capable of self-reflection. Just as rays of the sun are individual expressions of the sun itself, our individual sense of "I am" is an emanation of the infinite consciousness that permeates all things—what we might call God or the One-Life. This divine "I Am that I Am" is the ultimate consciousness from which all other consciousness—our individual "I am"—arises.

This perspective aligns with certain scientific research, which suggests that consciousness is a fundamental aspect of the universe, intricately woven into the very fabric of reality. It challenges the notion that consciousness is solely an emergent property of the brain, proposing instead that the brain acts as a receiver or conduit for consciousness to express itself in the physical world. According to this view, consciousness isn't confined to individual beings or living organisms—it extends to everything in the universe. Everything that exists possesses a degree of consciousness. This connects all things in the universe, creating a vast, interconnected web of awareness.

Thus, the "I Am that I Am" described in spiritual texts like Exodus isn't just a statement of existence; it's a declaration of the universal consciousness that permeates everything. It transcends time, form, and individuality, connecting all creation as expressions of the same infinite awareness. Our individual sense of "I am" is simply a localized manifestation of the all-encompassing "I Am that I Am."

This logical progression leads to the conclusion that "I Am" and consciousness are one and the same. The "I Am" is the purest, most fundamental expression of consciousness, and through recognizing this, we come to see that our individual awareness is inseparably linked to the universal consciousness that underlies all of existence.

Logos and Consciousness

One of the most fascinating concepts in understanding the nature of consciousness is the ancient Greek term *logos*. The word was first used around the sixth century BCE by the philosopher Heraclitus, who described *logos* as the underlying organizing principle governing the universe. To Heraclitus, *logos* was a form of cosmic intelligence that permeated all things, creating and sustaining the world in its intricate order.

Centuries later, in the early first century CE, the Hellenistic Jewish philosopher Philo of Alexandria expanded on this idea. Philo conceptualized *logos* as divine and transcendent, an eternal principle that underpins the entire universe. According to Philo, *logos* was a bridge between the material and the spiritual realms, a principle that could be grasped through contemplation, meditation, and mystical experiences. In Philo's view, *logos* was not only an intelligence but the very means by which the human mind could access divine reality.

This concept of *logos* finds a further evolution in the New Testament, particularly in the Gospel of John, where it is written: "In the beginning was the Word (*logos*), and the Word (*logos*) was with God, and the Word (*logos*) was God."[3] John paints a picture of creation where the *logos* existed before the universe came into being. He goes even further, suggesting that the *logos* was not only with God but was, in fact, God. John's portrayal of *logos* thus extends beyond Heraclitus's cosmic principle or Philo's divine intermediary.

If, as John asserts, the *logos* existed "in the beginning," it follows that it must have existed before the physical universe. And if it preceded matter and space, then it must also transcend time, since, as Einstein demonstrated, time only exists where there is matter and space. So, John's reference to the *logos* existing "in the beginning" signals a deeper truth: this divine organizing principle is not constrained by the limitations of time, space, or form. It is timeless and unchanging because it's ever-present in the *Now*.

John continues by stating that all things were made through *logos*, and without it, nothing came into being. The entire material universe arose from this *logos*, making it the very source from which reality emerges. As Paul, another biblical writer, later emphasizes, this *logos* is the invisible thread that holds the universe together, initiating creation and sustaining its existence.

John takes the concept further by suggesting that *logos* was embodied in the person of Jesus. Jesus reveals this profound truth when he declares, "Before Abraham was, I am." While "Abraham was" refers to a life confined within time and the physical world, the "I am" represents a timeless essence—the *zoe*-life. With these words, Jesus unveils his identity, not as a person or personality bound by time, space, and matter, but as the eternal "I Am," the very *logos*—the essence of being that transcends the material world.

It's easy to focus on Jesus solely in terms of his physical, human form. However, Jesus did not primarily identify with his personal, physical body. He understood that his body and mind were subject to the limitations of time, space, and matter, and he never claimed to have existed in physical form before his birth 2,000 years ago. Like all humans, Jesus grew from infancy to adulthood, learned through study, and acquired wisdom by listening to teachers and scholars. Yet, what sets Jesus apart is that he didn't identify with these temporary aspects of existence. He didn't see himself as merely flesh and bone, bound to change and decay; instead, he saw his true self as the timeless "I am"—pure, eternal consciousness.

So, when Jesus declared, "I am the way, the truth, and the life [zoe]," he wasn't speaking about his human identity or personality. The "I am" in his statement referred to his eternal spirit—consciousness, which he understood as his true self. Awakening within to the spirit, or pure consciousness, is the way to the Father because it's there that we are aware of our oneness with the "I Am that I Am." Jesus showed that we can truly know God only through inner awareness and awakening to this divine presence.

So, when the Gospel of John portrays Jesus as the *logos*, he tells us that Jesus knew himself as the "I am"—pure, divine consciousness— present at the foundation of the world. He recognized himself as the eternal spirit embodied in human form. In this way, Jesus became an archetype for humanity, showing us what it means to live in awareness of our deepest essence, united with the ultimate One-Life, which he referred to as his Father.

I share this insight into *logos* because it reveals a fascinating connection to modern quantum physics. As we mentioned earlier, some quantum physicists suggest that particles remain indeterminate until they are observed. Many take this further, arguing that the universe would remain formless and undetermined without consciousness. If this theory holds true, it reveals a parallel between spiritual wisdom and modern science: the *logos*—or the *I am*—is consciousness. Without consciousness, there is no form, no intelligence, no universe. Without consciousness, reality exists only as unrealized potential, a vast field of possibilities waiting to be brought into being. Consciousness, therefore, isn't merely a byproduct of the universe—it's the very force that brings everything into existence.

So, what does this mean for us? It reveals that consciousness is our core essence. It's not merely a part of us—it is who we are. Consciousness forms the foundation of our being, the timeless awareness that sustains our physical form and illuminates everything we experience.

While our individual consciousness is a mere drop in the vast ocean of universal consciousness, each drop is inseparably connected to the whole. In this way, we are all part of a grand narrative of existence, bound together through infinite consciousness—through God.

Ancient wisdom, echoed across cultures and eras, calls us to awaken to our oneness with God. Though our consciousness has been clouded and darkened by ego, when we enter a state of stillness and inner peace, we become aware of something beyond our personality and the physical world. We become attuned to the "I am" within the "I Am that I Am."

But how do we awaken to this reality? Interestingly, Philo of Alexandria, along with many spiritual traditions—and as we will later discover in Jesus's teachings—suggests that meditation is a path to becoming aware of our true essence. Meditation allows us to quiet the mind and move beyond the layers of ego, revealing our deeper identity as consciousness.

Throughout this book, I explore how meditation is a powerful tool for awakening to this inner dimension. For now, it is enough to say that the awareness of ourselves as the witnessing presence creates a profound shift in perspective. It allows us to step back from the drama of life and observe it with equanimity and wisdom. Through this awareness of our deepest self as consciousness, we discover the path to true peace and unity with all that exists.

You Are Not What You *Think* You Are

When I speak of consciousness as your true self, it's essential to understand that consciousness is not the same as your thoughts and emotions. Many people find it difficult to separate the two, so I emphasize this distinction. While the mind is essential to being human, it is not your true self. Your mind functions as a tool—a space where thoughts, emotions, and memories arise and take shape. It processes information and helps you navigate the world, but it's not the essence of who you are. In other words, you are not defined by what you think—you are the awareness behind those thoughts.

When you were born, your mind was like a blank slate—untouched by external influences. You had no narrative about who you were or what defined you. Yet, you still existed as "you," the same "you" that exists today.

This continuity exists because you are consciousness at the core of your being. Your true self is not the collection of thoughts and emotions that fill your mind. Rather, it is the inner awareness that perceives and processes these thoughts. As you grow, your mind becomes shaped by experiences, beliefs, and emotions. Over time, a mental and emotional image of who you are is constructed—built from lessons learned, societal influences, and personal experiences.

In this process, your thoughts begin to absorb your consciousness, making you believe that your thoughts are your identity. This creates a disconnect from the pure, simple consciousness that is your true essence. As a result, the innate state of peace and love within you—the essence of your being—gets obscured.

Now, you view your experiences through a mental framework shaped by past conditioning, often clouded by emotions like shame or fear. This framework solidifies into what is commonly referred to as the ego. The ego itself is not inherently negative, but its distorted perspective and constant mental chatter can obscure the stillness and clarity of your true self. This ego-based identity is like a distorted reflection in a funhouse mirror, an illusion that leads to suffering. Recognizing this illusion is the first step toward freedom.

The Egoic Mind

From the moment we are born, we are assigned labels and categories. A last name, a first name, and identifiers such as race, gender, and physical traits are given to us. As we grow, more labels are added—based on appearance, skills, intelligence, ethnicity, religion, and even our family's socioeconomic status. These labels shape the mental construct of who we think we are, contributing to the formation of our personality and giving rise to what we call the ego.

While I delve into the nature of the ego in greater depth in Chapter 6, I'll provide a brief overview here to contrast it with consciousness. The ego is a mind-created self, shaped by past experiences and driven by future aspirations. It constantly seeks fulfillment outside the present moment, leaving us perpetually dissatisfied, always chasing "something more" or "something different."

Beneath the surface of this egoic mind lie subtle feelings of either superiority or inferiority. Think about your relationships for a moment—do these feelings ever arise? If so, it's the ego at work. The ego thrives on comparison, whether we feel superior or inferior. It doesn't matter whether the outcome is positive or negative; the ego simply seeks to differentiate itself from others.

This constant comparison leads the ego to judge others, holding onto grudges and resentment when others make mistakes. This serves to mask the ego's own feelings of inadequacy and insecurity. It builds a sense of self, not by recognizing true worth, but by criticizing and distancing itself from others.

The ego also uses guilt to reinforce its identity. When we fall short of the standards set by our mind-created selves, we feel guilty. As we dwell on this guilt, it becomes part of our identity, reinforcing negative self-perception. Over time, we may even act in ways that align with this guilt-driven identity, further entrenching the belief that we are flawed.

Complaining is another tool the ego uses to strengthen itself. Whether in our thoughts or spoken aloud, we complain about circumstances, other people, tasks, past events, unmet expectations, or perceived injustices. In doing so, we create adversaries. The more we complain, the more conflict we generate, which the ego thrives on. It reinforces the idea of "me" versus "not me," deepening the ego's sense of separation.

This need for opposition extends beyond individuals to groups, nations, and religions, where collective egos are often strengthened by the presence of enemies. As the ego takes over, it monopolizes consciousness, shaping how we perceive reality and experience life. Fear and desire become the driving forces behind our thoughts and actions.

When consciousness is trapped in the egoic mind, it becomes unaware of its true nature, blind to genuine peace, love, and joy. In simpler terms, we lose touch with our deepest self. To rediscover our true nature is to find the key to freedom from the ego's grip, opening us to a life filled with peace, love, and joy.

The Unchanging Self

A healthy self-concept is essential for practical purposes —it helps you engage with others, focus on your goals, and set healthy boundaries. However, this self-concept is not your true self.

Your physical body changes over time, and your thoughts and emotions fluctuate. What remains constant is the unchanging awareness—the timeless witness, the "I am" that observes everything. This constancy is the continuity of consciousness, the ever-present self that exists in "Now," aware of both external events and internal processes, including thoughts and emotions.

The true self is the witnessing presence within you. Beyond your thoughts and emotions, you are the light of awareness that illuminates the world. Without this consciousness, there would be no experience of life or the world around us. Your true self is this consciousness—the inner light that manifests reality. It is the essence of who you are, the most authentic "I am."

By recognizing this unchanging essence, you move beyond the limits of the egoic mind. The shifting sands of thoughts, feelings, and physical changes can no longer define you.

Instead, you can rest in the vast ocean of consciousness that is your true nature, undisturbed by the waves of temporal experience. We return to the heart of awareness, the timeless "I am" that exists beyond the ego's fleeting identifications.

Why It Matters

Awareness of our true essence significantly alters our state of being. As we've explored, when we are no longer entirely absorbed by thoughts and emotions, we begin to experience life from a place of stillness. At first, the gap between our thoughts and consciousness may feel small. But as we deepen our inner awareness of the still, alive presence within us—the witnessing presence behind our thoughts—this space expands, and the egoic mind's control over our perception of reality gradually diminishes.

While the ego dominates our consciousness, the content of the ego dictates how we experience reality. But when we awaken to consciousness as our true self, we invite a new reality in which love and peace become the lens through which we see and interpret life. In this state, a deep inner wisdom guides our interactions and our approach to living.

We will expand on these ideas in later chapters. For now, let's rest in the understanding that our truest "I am" exists beyond thoughts and emotions. The primary purpose of human existence is to awaken to this consciousness—

spirit—our true self, which offers us a glimpse of reality through the eyes of God.

This shift in perception cultivates compassion, love, and forgiveness within our relationships, revealing the inter-connectedness of all things and the inherent value of every living being. As we align with this inner light, we embark on a path of wisdom and harmony, enriching our wellbeing and contributing to the healing and transfor-mation of the world around us.

5

THE VIBRATIONAL SIGNATURE

I magine a graphic artist sitting at their workstation, armed with a simple, mundane photograph. In their arsenal are countless filters, each with the power to dramatically transform the look and feel of the image. They could apply a vibrant, technicolor filter to create a joyful, lively ambiance or a somber black-and-white one to evoke a sense of nostalgia. Depending on its hues and contrasts, each filter creates a unique emotional tone, whether eerie, peaceful, dark, hellish, celestial, or anything in between.

Similarly, our life experiences act as filters on our consciousness, shaping how we see the world around us. At the core of these filters are our deep-rooted feelings, which develop even before we can think logically or form conscious memories. From the very beginning of life, long before we could reason or analyze, we were immersed in a world of feelings. These feelings become the primary filter through which we experience life.

As we grow, our emotional filter shapes how we perceive and interact with the world. This filter can either limit us or expand our potential, depending on the emotional patterns we carry. Each of us has a unique emotional tone —a personal frequency influencing how we experience life. This emotional tone creates what may be called our *vibrational signature*, which is different for everyone. It's like an energetic imprint that reflects our individual emotional state. This unique vibrational signature not only shapes how we see the world but also affects how others perceive and respond to us. It's not just a metaphor —it's a natural, palpable energy that others can sense, even without any spoken words.

Research in neuro-cardiology has revealed that the heart's electromagnetic field is incredibly powerful—up to five thousand times stronger than the brain's.[1] This field extends beyond our body and resonates with our emotions, influencing us and the people around us. For instance, studies have shown that the heartbeats of a mother and child can synchronize, as can those of individuals deeply connected in conversation. This heart-based communication creates a subtle but profound connection between people, even before body language or words are exchanged.

Imagine walking into a room after a heated argument. Although the argument is over, you can still feel the tension in the air. Your own body responds, perhaps with a racing heart or a knot in your stomach. This is an example of how emotional energy lingers and affects the atmosphere around us. Conversely, imagine being in the presence of someone who is deeply peaceful and centered. Their calm energy affects you, causing your muscles to relax and your mind to quiet down. The energy they project shifts the emotional tone of the environment, drawing others into their sphere of tranquility.

Over time, our consistent emotional tone becomes the unique filter through which we experience life, shaping our reality. In other words, our vibrational signature, formed by our habitual emotional state, influences the people and experiences we attract. For instance, a person filled with joy and gratitude will likely draw in positive, uplifting experiences, while someone dwelling in anger or negativity may attract conflict and dissatisfaction. Our emotional filter acts like a magnet, pulling in people and situations that resonate with our internal state.

Spiritual texts often describe this vibrational signature as our "soul." In Judeo-Christian scripture, the term "soul," or *psychē* in Greek, refers to the personal, emotional, and intellectual aspects of a human being. It is considered the seat of our thoughts, emotions, and desires. While closely related, the soul is distinct from the spirit. Both terms are connected to the idea of breath —*psychē* for the soul and *pneuma* for the spirit. However, the spirit, or *pneuma*, represents the divine life—pure consciousness—while the soul is what forms when a filter of our unique emotional tone is placed upon that consciousness. This filter shapes how we perceive the world and the emotional tone we project to those around us.

In this way, the soul can be seen as the vital breath, the essence we individually exhale into the world—a reflection of our inner emotional landscape. It is our unique vibrational signature that influences how we experience life. While the spirit is like the universal breath or wind we inhale, sustaining all life, the soul represents the distinct emotional and energetic tone that emanates from each of us, shaping the reality we create and experience.

To transform the filter through which we perceive the world, we must awaken to the spirit within us— consciousness itself. By recognizing that we are not defined by the shifting thoughts and emotions that make up our temporary experiences, we can shift the emotional filter that shapes our reality. Awakening to the timeless, formless "I am" within us allows us to move beyond the limitations of our emotional filters and access a state of inner peace, creativity, and wisdom.

When we align with this deeper state of consciousness, the filter through which we experience life changes. Inner tranquility and clarity become the foundation of our experience, and we begin to attract a new reality that reflects the universe's infinite wisdom and creativity. In this awakened state, we are no longer limited by the filters of fear, guilt, or negativity. Instead, we live from a place of profound inner stillness, where the external world mirrors the peace we hold within.

The Collective Atmosphere

On a broader scale, society's emotional vibration is the aggregate of its individuals' emotional states. When a substantial number of people collectively experience similar emotions, it can generate a collective vibrational signature influencing the overall mood, energy, and even societal events and outcomes. For instance, in countries suffering from the repercussions of war, I've detected a pervasive sense of pain in the collective consciousness. In contrast, a palpable sense of greed is discernible in other places.

Many years ago, I had the opportunity to join a promotional trip to Israel with a group of twelve people. Each day, we experienced something unique and different. One day, our guide informed us that we were scheduled to spend a half-day on a Kibbutz located by the serene Sea of Galilee. Initially, I was less than enthusiastic about the idea and even contemplated ways to evade this part of the trip. Despite my reluctance, I ended up going.

What I hadn't anticipated was how deeply this seemingly mundane visit would affect me. Even now, I remember the experience with astonishing clarity. That Kibbutz radiated a profound sense of community and belonging. The people there emanated an energy of peace, undeniably influenced by the surrounding natural beauty and the slow rhythm of their lives. This environment fostered strong community bonds, cultivated an appreciation for simplicity, and prioritized environmental sustainability. Unexpectedly, what I assumed would be the least exciting part of the trip was the most impactful. It was an experience that touched me profoundly and has remained with me to this day.

As we see here, not only do we as individuals carry our own unique vibrational signature that affects the world around us, but when a substantial number of people share a similar emotional atmosphere, it impacts the environment on a larger scale. It draws people together who resonate with the same emotional tone, creating what could be called "collective soul ties." These soul ties extend beyond just two individuals, forming energetic bonds within groups or communities. This shared emotional frequency amplifies the collective experience, further shaping the reality of everyone involved.

This leads to important questions: How can we transform our emotional tone? And how can our collective atmosphere evolve to foster not only individual wellbeing but also a cultural shift on a broader scale?

Decoding Our State of Being and Its Impact on Reality

We all relate to different ideas and terminology; sometimes, certain concepts can cause some to tune out, misunderstand, or feel confused. So, let's approach it from a different angle that may bring added clarity—our state of being.

When we refer to ourselves as "human beings," we acknowledge our true essence as consciousness housed within a physical form. As human beings, we are aware of our essence within the confines of our bodies. When we discuss our "state of being," we are talking about the state or condition of our embodied consciousness. Even though we are all human beings, our individual states vary significantly.

At the core of your state of being is the interplay between your brain and heart. Emotions originate as signals in the brain, often influenced by your thoughts and perceptions of the world. These signals are communicated to your body, generating physical sensations, particularly in the heart.

These physical and emotional responses form the foundation of your state of being. For example, the mind fixates on fear or worry under intense stress, while the body responds with tightness or discomfort. This creates a state of being marked by unease. Conversely, when you feel calm or joyful, the brain and heart align in harmony, fostering a state of peace and openness.

Your state of being not only shapes how you feel internally but also radiates outward, influencing your life experience and interactions with others. This helps explain why two people might respond differently to the same situation. One may feel overwhelmed and react with anxiety, while the other sees a challenge and responds with excitement. Their thoughts, emotions, and physiological responses interact to create distinct states of being, which in turn affect their reality.

A Lesson from the Radio

Much like a radio, we human beings can tune into and broadcast different frequencies along the electromagnetic spectrum. Imagine for a moment that your mind is the radio receiver, and your state of being corresponds to a specific radio frequency.

Every radio station operates on a distinct frequency. When we adjust the radio dial, we tune into different radio stations, each broadcasting its unique content. Similarly, our mind can tune into various electromagnetic frequencies, which we subsequently broadcast through our state of being.

Say you're tuned into the "anxiety" frequency. You'll start broadcasting worry and distress and likely attract circumstances that amplify these feelings. Conversely, if you adjust your dial to tune into the "peace" frequency, you'll start radiating tranquility, attracting situations that resonate with this peaceful state.

Returning to our earlier reflection, think of your soul as both a receiver and a broadcaster. What you send out into the universe depends on the frequency you're tuned into —your emotions, thoughts, and overall state of being.

Like a radio wave, your unique energy or vibrational signature is broadcast from your heart, affecting the world around you and shaping your reality according to the spiritual and emotional frequencies you're aligned with.

When you're tuned into higher frequencies, such as love, peace, and joy, your heart broadcasts these uplifting energies, attracting people and experiences that reflect these positive states. But if you're aligned with lower frequencies like fear, anger, or resentment, you send out similar energy, drawing in experiences and people that mirror those challenging emotions.

If you want to experience a different reality, you need to align your state of being with higher frequencies. This shift changes the energy you project, not only transforming your interactions with the world but also reshaping your reality in a more positive and harmonious way.

This insight brings us back to the intuitive wisdom of Jesus and his revolutionary perspective on perceiving reality differently. He taught us about cocreating a new reality with God—a reality capable of transforming not just individual lives, but also the world. This profound teaching encourages us to first silence the noisy static of the various frequencies that swirl around us and, from there, tune our personal "radio" to the frequency of the kingdom of God, fostering a state of being that aligns with love, peace, and joy, thereby helping us cocreate a better world for all. Before we consider this wisdom of Jesus and his groundbreaking teaching on the kingdom of God, we need to understand the perspective of the language and culture of his time.

Approaching the Wisdom of Jesus Through His Semitic Culture

The mother tongue of Jesus was Aramaic, which is closely related to Hebrew. Despite the New Testament's Greek composition, Jesus would have seldom interacted with anyone who spoke Greek, save for the societal elite who collaborated with the Romans. Jesus must, therefore, have primarily communicated in Aramaic for people to comprehend him. Indeed, many scholars hold the view that at least two of the Gospels were initially written in Aramaic before being translated into Greek to reach a broader audience.

To truly grasp how Jesus's teachings would have resonated with the inhabitants of the regions where he preached, it's crucial to consider the cultural and linguistic context of his time. For instance, Jesus frequently used figures of speech characteristic of Semitic languages, such as Aramaic, Hebrew, and Arabic. Contrasting with contemporary English, these expressions were more poetic and vivid, deploying rich imagery and symbolic language to convey meaning.

Furthermore, Semitic languages employed a stylistic device known as "parallelism," wherein the second line of a sentence echoed the first. They also utilized intricate grammatical structures and diverse verb forms to convey delicate nuances of meaning that are less common in modern English.

The lifestyle of the Semitic people during Jesus's time was also markedly different from ours today. All Semitic communities, including those Jesus interacted with, were traditionally nomadic, wandering across deserts, mountains, and other landscapes in pursuit of resources like water and food for survival. This way of life fostered a deep connection to the earth, as their survival hinged on their capacity to navigate and live in harmony with their environment.

Unlike modern Western societies that focus on individualism, Semitic cultures were rooted in a deep sense of community and interdependence. For them, life was viewed as part of a larger interconnected system, where everything influenced and relied on each other. This worldview was reflected in their language, filled with expressions that highlighted this mutual connection. With this in mind, let's dive into the teachings of Jesus and see how they can help us transform our emotional tone and shift our collective atmosphere, fostering not only individual wellbeing but also driving broader cultural change.

What is *Really* The Kingdom of God?

When we study the wisdom of Jesus, a recurring theme emerges that dominates his teachings. Throughout the

Gospels, the notion of the kingdom of God or the kingdom of Heaven is a constant thread, serving as the main backdrop for all Jesus said.

For centuries, theologians have debated what Jesus meant by the kingdom. What was Jesus referring to when he spoke about the kingdom of God? In Aramaic, the kingdom of God is *malkuta d'Alaha*. *Malkuta*, which we translate as "kingdom," has a feminine gender, making "queendom" a potentially more precise translation.[2] However, focusing on the gendered form of the word overlooks its true meaning. *Malkuta* stems from ancient nomadic cultures of the Middle Eastern deserts, evoking the image of a heart-centered visionary leader guiding their people with passion and the energy to bring their vision to life. It conveys a sense of collective empowerment—"We can do this." The leader inspires their people to rise up and move forward with confidence and shared purpose, much like the 2008 Barack Obama political campaign that rallied behind the energizing slogan, "Yes, we can."

Applied to personal lives, *malkuta* represents the inner voice that affirms, "I can."[3] As we journey through life, we encounter defining moments that evoke this affirmation: "I can drive." "I can purchase that home." Yet, the purity of this "I can" often gets overshadowed by ego, leading us into life's challenges. Hence, when Jesus speaks of the kingdom of God, he alludes to the divine "I can" manifesting through us—a higher form of wisdom and creativity guiding us to lead our most enriched lives.

In one of his teachings, Jesus says, "Seek first the kingdom of God... and all these things will be added to you."[4] By "things," he referred to everything we need in our human experience. When we seek the divine *malkuta*—the universal, inner sense of "I can"—everything we need flows naturally into our lives. By aligning ourselves with this flow of wisdom and creativity, we create the space for abundance and fulfillment to come our way.

Jesus also makes it clear that the kingdom of God is non-physical, existing beyond space, time, and matter. Consider his words, "The kingdom of God is within you."[5] In the Aramaic language, "within" also means "among," hinting at a kingdom unbound by physical limitations. It's a gateway to our most profound potential, where the clamor of division and strife fall away, leaving a spiritual melody that resonates with the universal truth of inter-connectedness.

Jesus's insights transform everyday living into an extraordinary life. He perceived a spiritual reality—a frequency, if you will—that brought forth a life of abundance and harmony when people were attuned to it. He saw the burdens and anxieties of the people around him and offered an elegant, timeless, and universal solution. By harmonizing with the kingdom—a resonance imbued with peace, love, and joy—the divine "I can" awakens within, bestowing us with a transcending wisdom and creativity. It's as if, when our hearts synchronize with this divine wavelength, life's essentials gravitate toward us with the same inexorable pull that attracts metal to a magnet.

This isn't a mystical abstraction. It's an actionable principle that takes us beyond our conventional understanding of reality. Imagine your consciousness as a tuning fork, vibrating harmoniously with God. As you resonate with these higher frequencies, your very being becomes a conduit for the extraordinary, a nexus where human potential and divine purpose converge.

Our unique vibrational signature thus becomes a beacon, drawing from a cosmic field that defies definition yet is ripe with possibilities. It's an uncharted sea of opportunity waiting for explorers brave enough to set sail. When we enter this dimension, we step into a garden of existence where our deepest intentions blossom into reality with a grace that seems almost otherworldly. We attune to Presence that whispers the universe's secrets into our hearts, guiding us along a transcending path illuminated by grace, compassion, and boundless love.

So, the kingdom of God, as described by Jesus, is not a lofty ideal but a practical guide, an extraordinary lens through which we can view our lives. It's a way of being that transforms the mundane into the extraordinary and opens doors to a world where, as Jesus promised, "all things are possible."[6]

Revisiting "Born Again"

One of Jesus's most renowned yet frequently miscon-strued statements is recorded in the Gospel of John. Here, Jesus converses with Nicodemus, a Pharisee and a member of the Sanhedrin, the Jewish governing council. Nicodemus visited Jesus at night, possibly to avoid being seen by his peers, and recognized Jesus as a teacher sent from God. Jesus then informed Nicodemus that *he could not see the kingdom of God unless he was born again.*[7]

The phrase "born again," as employed by Jesus in his native Aramaic, is *metiyled men d'riysh*, translating to "born from the first or original source."[8] Here, the Semitic roots of *riysh* indicate "Beginning," as also referred to in the opening verses of John's Gospel account. This suggests a state of formlessness, emptiness, and tranquility beyond the confines of time and space—a pure state of conscious-ness, as discussed in the preceding chapter. Essentially, Jesus conveyed that we must return to the First, the Begin-ning—a state of pure inner peace where we merely observe, free from any mental framework that interprets and categorizes the physical world.

Consider this. At the moment of your birth, you were purely conscious and aware, devoid of any mental labels or judgments about your identity. You existed without any internal emotional story or self-concept. For instance, as a newborn, you weren't fretting about whether you'd be fed the next day or feeling remorseful for crying too much the previous day. You held no speculations about life five years ahead or concerns that a minor stomach ache might hint at a larger issue. There was no trace of anxiety, worry, or guilt. You were solely in an unconditioned state of alertness, rooted in the present. You were the very essence of presence, illuminating the world around you.

By revisiting this state of egoless existence, Jesus suggested that we could achieve freedom and "see the kingdom of God," as recounted by John. In Aramaic, the term Jesus used was *d'nechzé malkuta d'Alaha*. The Aramaic term for "see" here is *nechzé*, and it has a root meaning that denotes a sudden inner vision or mystical experience, often attained through contemplation and meditation. It's evident from the Aramaic root text that Jesus wasn't referring to a theoretical belief here, but a genuine, profound experience. Jesus suggested that by contemplating the mystery of the formless Beginning—the eternal consciousness that predates creation—our understanding would be illuminated, leading us to perceive the *malkuta d'Alaha*—the kingdom of God.

In essence, to "see" meant reaching a state of inner stillness, free from the relentless internal dialogue, and simply becoming aware. If you have meditated in silence and momentarily arrived at a place where you are just conscious of your breath or inner energy field, you understand what I'm implying. Even a brief pause to become aware of the energy field in your hands frees you from the ego-driven mind. You are reverting to that original state before a conceptual self-belief existed. You are simply alert—conscious without mental noise.

It's from this ascending state of internal peace that we become aware of the kingdom of God, according to Jesus. Only when we return to a nondual consciousness, devoid of ego—even if for a fleeting moment—can we perceive the kingdom of God—God's "I can"—through an inner vision.

Once our heart finds peace and our mind rests in the *now*, the gates to the kingdom of God swing open. When we enter, it signifies a metamorphosis in our state of being or vibrational signature. Our heart resonates with peace, and we deeply love everything. In this transformed state, we access a dimension of existence where the limitless possibilities of God become tangible.

Could Jesus have alluded to this when he spoke of having the God-kind of faith that moves mountains? With such a faith, the boundaries restricting what can be achieved dissolve, and the realm of possibility stretches as wide as the universe's infinite wisdom. An inner vision, firmly grounded in peace and love, that sees beyond material constraints, beckons us into a domain teeming with infinite possibilities. We are invited to walk in this spiritual landscape, guided by a timeless wisdom that transcends our ordinary understanding.

It's Not What It Seems to Be

Let's delve into another teaching of Jesus that amplifies what we have just discussed—a wisdom that echoes throughout his itinerant life and the pages of the Gospels, urging us to "repent, for the kingdom of God is at hand."[9] Shrouded in mystery and often misunderstood, these words carry a timeless truth far removed from traditional interpretations that have shaped centuries of thought.

The term "repent" in the Semitic language of Jesus does not mean remorse or penance in the way many modern readers might understand it. It doesn't demand a sorrowful regret for past wrongdoings or a plea for forgiveness. Instead, it invites us to return to the beginning, to an origin untouched by time, judgments, or societal constructs. In the original Aramaic, the word for "repent" is *tub,* meaning "to return" or "to turn." It's about changing course, refocusing, and rediscovering the essence of our true self, free from the layers of cultural conditioning and personal history that often obscure our perception.

"At hand" is not merely a reference to proximity in time or space. It's a gentle whisper, telling us that something profound is accessible now, all around and within us. The kingdom of God, as Jesus described, is not a remote or futuristic realm but the divine "I can"—a reality of higher wisdom and creativity that is present and accessible through a shift in awareness.

So, when Jesus urges us to "repent, for the kingdom of God is at hand," he's not calling for guilt or self-abasement, but a profound transformation of our state of being. He's inviting us to wake up to the divine reality that permeates everything, to recognize the sacredness in ourselves and in all life, and to live in alignment with this higher truth.

It's an invitation to release the shackles of ego, fear, and misunderstanding and embrace a vision of life filled with peace, joy, and love. It's a call to step out of the mental constructs that divide us and enter a state of unity and harmony with the whole of existence. In other words, it's a way for our vibrational signature—our state of being—to be transformed so we attract a new reality based on inner tranquility and the infinite wisdom and creativity of the universe.

A Day at Robben Island

Before we move on, I'd like to share an evocative story that beautifully illustrates the transformative power that a metamorphosis of our state of being can wield in shaping our reality. One of my most meaningful and unforgettable days occurred while visiting Robben Island outside Cape Town, South Africa.

Upon arriving at Robben Island, an overpowering sense of history washed over me. The ferry's engines hummed a somber note as we approached the place that once held Nelson Mandela captive for eighteen of his twenty-seven years in prison. The atmosphere itself seemed to vibrate with the echoes of the past.

Standing inside Mandela's cell was a humbling experience. The stark, confined space resonated with a palpable emotional tone, a vibration that spoke of resilience, introspection, and transformation. It was hard to fathom how a man could endure such hardship and confinement, yet emerge not with bitterness, but with love and forgiveness.

Mandela's earlier life was not all love. Instead, he was a young man filled with conflict and anger. A struggle against an oppressive system marked his formative years, but it was within the walls of prison that his true transformation began.

During those long years on Robben Island, Mandela underwent a profound metamorphosis. He found a way to "return to the beginning," aligning with a state of being that transcended his immediate circumstances. Through meditation, reflection, and deep inner work, he reshaped his mindset, letting go of anger in favor of understanding and replacing resentment with forgiveness.

This shift in his emotional tone, his vibrational signature, resonates with the teachings of love and forgiveness that echo the kingdom of God we discussed earlier. Mandela's transformation was a living embodiment of that divine wisdom. He understood that true power lay not in domination, but in embracing the interconnectedness of all beings.

Mandela's newfound awareness was not confined to his inner world. It radiated outward, affecting those around him and ultimately transforming an entire nation. His forgiveness and love were not mere words, but potent energies that shifted the collective vibrational signature of

South Africa. Upon his release and through his eventual rise to the highest office in the land, he didn't seek revenge but urged reconciliation. He understood that healing a divided nation required a higher vibration, a universal love that could dissolve the artificial barriers of race and creed.

The impossibility of ending apartheid, the unimaginable feat of a peaceful transition to democracy, became possible through Mandela's embodiment of a higher spiritual reality. His leadership reflected a universal truth: When we align with peace, love, and a sense of oneness, we tap into a dimension where limitless possibilities unfold.

His story vividly illustrates the timeless wisdom we've explored—that our feelings shape our reality and that by consciously aligning with higher spiritual frequencies, we can create a reality filled with peace, wisdom, and compassion. It's a lesson that transcends history and geography, touching the core of our shared human experience. It's a reminder that the kingdom of God is not just a spiritual concept, but a practical, living reality accessible to all who tune into it.

Now that you know you can change your state of being and create a new, harmonious reality, profound questions arise: Why does this transformation seem so tricky and inconceivable for so many people? Is it simply a lack of will or something more profound that keeps us tethered to old patterns, inhibiting our growth and fulfillment?

And where does our own metamorphosis, this profound alteration of our inner state, begin? How do we embark on this ascending path, unlocking doors we may not even realize confined us? Stay tuned as we continue to explore these questions.

6

THE BARRIER OF THE EGO

The path to crafting a new reality is sometimes akin to navigating a maze—a complex puzzle filled with twists and turns, obscured by barriers, primarily constructed by our very minds. It brings to mind the wise words of Rumi: "Your task is not to seek for love, but merely to seek and find all the barriers within yourself that you have built against it."[1]

These barriers are not simply fortifications against love but walls and moats that divide us from our true self, cutting off our connection to a profound sense of wholeness. Rumi's message carries a special weight, urging us to dismantle these barriers so that we may find our true self and awaken to the love, peace, and wisdom that lies dormant within us, just waiting to be unveiled.

But what exactly are these barriers? What stands between us and our ability to perceive reality and experience life through inner wholeness? The primary obstacle is the ego. This isn't to say the ego is an outright villain, as it plays its part in helping us navigate life. Yet, its tendency to seek identity, to build itself up by differentiating itself from others, emerges as a significant barrier to genuine happiness and fulfillment.

Envision the ego not as a guardian angel but as a skilled architect of illusions, erecting walls and fortresses, not to safeguard, but rather to isolate us from our own potential, other people, and the vast, limitless expanse of possibility.

A Humbling Experience

Allow me to recall a humbling moment from years ago. On a seemingly ordinary day, I found myself visiting a car dealership. The lease on my car had approached its end, and I was hunting for a good deal on my next vehicle. What unfolded, however, was far from an ordinary transaction. It was a lesson, a mirror reflecting back to me one of the most profound barriers to fostering wholeness: the ego.

The ego likes to win because it equates winning with strength. The simple act of looking for a new car revealed how the ego, in its quest for victory, acts as a barrier to awakening our deepest essence.

As I drove into the dealership, a familiar figure greeted me —the same older gentleman who had leased me the car I was about to return. As his name suggested, we shared a

Scandinavian heritage, but our similarities seemed to end there.

Upon his inquiry about my satisfaction with my current car, I revealed my disappointment with the GPS's voice-command feature. His surprise hinted at subtle blame-shifting, implying that the issue was not with the car but with my ability to use it properly.

In this brief conversation, a subtle undercurrent was at play. Our logical mind processes information at a limited pace, while our hearts quickly pick up on the energies and intentions behind spoken words. The car dealer's insinuation felt like an assault on my aptitude. The ego, feeling attacked, was roused into defense.

Armed with the knowledge of other people having shared the same complaint about the GPS, I was initially inclined to recount some of those instances. But whether it was the prospect of a good deal or a moment of self-restraint, I held my tongue and decided to demonstrate the issue instead.

I commanded the GPS to navigate to La Jolla, a nearby community, only for it to identify a location in Idaho, over 2,000 miles away. As expected, the salesperson's defense grew, attributing the issue to my accent. His comments triggered a rush of emotions within me—remnants of an immigrant's struggle, echoes of derogatory remarks from my initial days in Canada, and the daunting process of becoming a US citizen. The ego in me seized this moment to launch a counterattack, skillfully turning the issue into a critique of Acura's ability to cater to people like me and their seeming disinterest in adapting to immigrants.

The salesperson was left speechless, and, for a brief moment, I felt a false sense of victory—a validation of the ego. But what did this "victory" achieve? Did it secure me a good deal? Did it leave me with a pleasant feeling? In the aftermath, all that remained was a trail of negativity, wasted time and energy, a strained relationship, and a stark reminder of how our shared divine union was overlooked in the heat of the moment.

Such moments, when the ego seeks validation, can stack up over time, forming unconscious patterns of regrets, anxieties, and even illness. It is vital to remember that our experiences are not merely cognitive, but are also encoded in our cellular memory, affecting our wellbeing.

This incident at the dealership was not just a lesson, but a clarion call—a vivid illustration of how the ego, with its insatiable hunger to be right, to win, can erect formidable barriers that hinder us from crafting a new reality, founded on peace, genuine love, and compassion.

So, what exactly is this ego that builds such barriers to our wellbeing, and how might we begin to dismantle these barricades?

What Is Ego?

The word "ego" comes from ancient Greek, where it simply means "I" or "self." Over time, many spiritual and philosophical traditions have contrasted this ego-self with a higher or true self, often linking the latter to a deeper spiritual reality or pure consciousness. For example, in Christian mysticism, the ego is often seen as the *false self*—rooted in pride, selfishness, and a sense of separation from God. It's the part of us that clings to selfish desires and fears. Mystics like Meister Eckhart also spoke of a "divine spark" within us, our *true self* that is one with God.

According to this view, our spiritual journey involves "dying to self"—or the ego—to awaken to the divine presence within, ultimately becoming aware of unity with God through love and surrender—a letting go of the ego's need for control and superiority, yielding instead to the deeper, unconditional love that flows from being one with God.

Another way to understand the ego-self is as the personal identity we've constructed over time—the "I" or "me" that navigates the world. Unlike our true self, which is unconditioned and represents the pure "I am," without anything added, the ego-self is shaped by the environment we grew up in, the people we interact with, and the cultural norms around us. Essentially, the ego is the conditioned self, formed by our experiences and the emotional wounds we've gathered along the way. We can think of the ego as a jigsaw puzzle, with each piece representing a fragment of our past, carefully assembled in our subconscious. Even though this puzzle may be incomplete or disjointed, it forms the image we hold of ourselves and influences how we live our lives.

Another key difference between the true self and the ego-self is that the true self exists fully in the present moment, while the ego-self builds its identity from thoughts rooted in the past and seeks significance in what it might achieve in the future. The ego-self is rarely content with the present, constantly judging our experiences and storing them in the subconscious, only to use them to shape our expectations for the future.

At the core of the ego lies a powerful need to define and strengthen our sense of self through external attachments. This need is driven by the ego's desire to stand out and be seen as superior to others, to assert its rightness, and to push others into the wrong. To achieve this sense of superiority and significance, the ego seeks out objects, roles, and beliefs to latch onto and incorporate into its identity. This process is known as identification, a mechanism deeply rooted in the mind.

The word "identification" comes from the Latin words *idem,* meaning "same," and *facere,* meaning "to make." When we identify with something—whether it's a possession, a role, or a belief—we make it the same as or part of ourselves, weaving it into the fabric of our identity. In this way, the ego is a thought pattern rooted in these attachments, which we mistakenly associate with who we are. This mental activity gradually overshadows consciousness, leading us to confuse our thoughts with our true self. René Descartes famously alluded to this misconception with the statement, "I think, therefore I am."

However, "I am" precedes thoughts. Our true "I am" is the eternal, unchanging witness to our thoughts, not the thoughts themselves. The ego, then, is the self that the mind identifies with—essentially a mental construct, not the spirit, which remains untouched and pure, observing the dance of thoughts from the stillness of our true essence.

Before we explore the ego more practically, it's important to clarify a key point. We often use terms like "my true self" or "my ego" for simplicity, but this language doesn't fully capture the reality. The ego isn't something we actually possess—if it were, who would be the one possessing it? It could not be our true self because the timeless "I am" simply exists. It doesn't possess the ego because doing so would contradict its nature of being free and unattached.

Similarly, consciousness isn't something we own, as that would imply it's separate from us. In truth, consciousness is the essence of who we are. We use words like "my" or "our" to help express these ideas, even though the concepts themselves are deeper than what language can fully convey.

As we awaken to our true essence as consciousness, this understanding becomes clearer and more grounded in experience. We start to feel less attached to our thoughts and emotions, seeing them as temporary, almost distant. Our true essence is the witnessing presence—the "I am"—that observes these egoic thoughts and emotions without identifying with them.

The Ego's Framework: How It Operates and Separates

Understanding the ego can seem complex, but it becomes more apparent if we consider its two elements: content and structure.[2] These two elements can be likened to a house: the structure is the foundational aspect that remains constant across all houses, whereas the content is the unique individuality of each home.

The structure of a house—its foundation, walls, and roof—remains essentially the same for every building, regardless of where it is or who owns it. Similarly, the structure of the ego is the same for every person. It forms the underlying basis on which the individual egoic identity is built.

However, just as every house is uniquely different in terms of color, size, building materials, and design—the content, so too is the content of the ego. Our personal experiences, beliefs, values, thoughts, and emotions make up the content of the ego, setting each of us apart from the rest.

To illustrate, let's take the allegorical story of Adam and Eve in the Garden of Eden. In this story, their compulsion (the structure of the ego) to enhance their sense of self led them to consume the fruit (the content) that they thought would make them wise (add something to their sense of self).

What are the characteristics that define this universal structure of the ego? One of the core traits is that the ego is most enhanced and strengthened by contrast, by how it stands out or apart from others—how I am different from you. This requires a continuum of opposites, a sense of polarity or duality. This duality is clearly demonstrated in the story of Adam and Eve, where the continuum is between good and evil.

How does the ego navigate these dualities in daily life? Interestingly, it is most strengthened when it perceives itself as having enemies. Here are a few ways in which the ego creates adversaries:

Comparisons: The ego constantly compares itself to others, leading to a subtle feeling of either inferiority or superiority in relationships. These comparisons often manifest as subtle feelings, such as "I'm smarter than my siblings" or "I have had many more bad breaks in my life than they have." Another such juxtaposition might be "My political or religious worldview is superior to most others" or "My people are more morally upright than those people." These thoughts and feelings often go unnoticed because the ego has absorbed our consciousness.

Judgment: When feelings of insecurity arise, the ego often responds by judging those who evoke these feelings. Even if the person has done nothing wrong, the ego may perceive them as a threat and seek to identify their faults. This negative judgment acts as a mechanism to bring them lower on the continuum of right and wrong, thus enhancing our own egoic sense of self.

Complaining: Closely related to judgment, complaining about others strengthens the ego by creating negative narratives about their identities. By focusing on what we perceive as negative aspects of another's identity, we reinforce our own positive self-image.

Insisting on Being Right: The ego thrives on maintaining its own correctness and the wrongness of others. This is particularly noticeable in areas of firmly held beliefs such as politics or religion. It's why we see such varied and often polarizing viewpoints in society.

Resentment: The ego holds onto resentment for perceived wrongs done by others. This resentment not only allows the ego to feel superior. It also offers a reason to be angry or offended and to justify our actions while condemning others.

Grievances: The ego also holds onto grievances, long-standing resentments that cannot be easily forgotten or forgiven. These grievances create unconscious scars in our hearts, engendering constant negative feelings toward the person or situation associated with them.

These patterns of comparison, judgment, complaining, insistence on being right, resentment, and grievance are all subconscious strategies the ego employs to strengthen itself and create separation between "me" and "others." They are the building blocks of the ego's structure, deeply ingrained within our subconscious.

These strategies temporarily boost our ego but ultimately result in unhappiness and suffering. This is because, when we place others on the "bad" side of the spectrum, it generates tension, stress, anxiety, and even depression. Our minds become filled with negative chatter about what others have or have not done to or for us, which leads to unhappiness.

Egoic Content: The Ever-Changing Face of Self-Identity

We've established that the structure of the ego is a universal aspect, common to every individual. However, the content, which refers to what we identify with to augment our sense of self, is unique for each person. This content, or personal identification, is shaped by environmental influences, upbringing, and the surrounding culture.

What's fascinating about this egoic content is its inherent contradictions. Our egos are like chameleons, changing desires based on the situation and often seemingly unsure about what they really want. Their main constant is a stubborn resistance to living in the now.

A hallmark of the ego is its insatiable appetite for more. It thrives not on having, but on wanting. The chase energizes the ego far more than the catch. This perpetual yearning for something new to reinforce our sense of worth reflects the values assigned by others, such as family, popular culture, religious institutions, or even counter-culture groups like gangs or organized crime rings. This relentless pursuit often leads us on a merry chase, seeking validation in possessions or accolades that, in the end, might not truly fulfill us. It's a quest driven by external approval rather than inner contentment, revealing the ego's knack for dressing up desire as need, keeping us forever on the hunt for the next thing that might make us feel complete.

The marketing industry is a master at leveraging the ego's deep-seated desire to boost its importance and identity. It cleverly uses cultural benchmarks of what's considered valuable to make us desire certain products. By associating brands with celebrity endorsements or symbols of luxury, beauty, and other enviable traits, marketers sell us on the idea that owning these items will elevate our self-image or social standing, feeding into the ego's hunger for recognition.

The often-high prices of these products make them even more desirable. If these items were universally accessible, they would lose their psychological appeal, and their value would be reduced to their material worth—likely a fraction of the retail price. This dynamic shows how adeptly the marketing industry can manipulate our desires, turning wants into needs and luxury into a perceived necessity for enhancing our social persona.

It's worth noting that the ego is resourceful. If one form of identification is eliminated, it quickly latches onto another. The actual object of identification matters little to the ego as long as it reaffirms its existence. Even anti-consumerism or anti-private ownership sentiments can replace materialistic identification, allowing the ego to continue its patterns of self-importance and judgment.

The specific elements or concepts that individuals identify with can vary considerably, depending on personal factors such as age, gender, income, social class, current trends, and cultural context. However, typical anchors for identification include attributes like intelligence, attractiveness, wealth, status or fame, religious and political convictions, morality, and integrity.

Intriguingly, not all content we identify with might initially seem to strengthen the ego. For instance, an individual might sometimes feel like a failure due to setbacks in life. In such cases, the egoic mind quickly adopts the identity of a victim, blaming unfavorable circumstances or "evil" individuals. This blaming of others eases feelings of inadequacy the ego might have about not being, having, or doing enough, thereby strengthening the ego's hold on us.

These egoic patterns of enhancing self-worth through content take on many complex forms. For example, in my confrontation with the auto sales representative, I swiftly shifted from feeling victimized by perceived insults to attempting to reclaim my worth by trying to demonstrate intelligence through skillfully making my case. While an individual might be more prone to a particular form of egoic enhancement, it often fluctuates, depending on what might best address the situation at hand.

The Many Faces of the Ego

Imagine a woman named Deborah arriving at her workplace one Monday morning. As she steps into the office, her ego instantly comes into play. She spots a new face—a colleague recently recruited. The colleague, radiant in her youthful confidence and stylish clothing, immediately triggers Deborah's ego. It begins the process of comparison.

Deborah's ego recalls her early days and the energy and enthusiasm she brought to her role. It reminds her of the many years she's put into this company, the countless hours of hard work, and the promotions earned. Deborah may feel a surge of superiority in response to this newcomer, based on her experience and longevity within the company.

However, simultaneously, the ego can play a different tune. Seeing the newcomer's youthful energy, innovative ideas, and the attention she's attracting, Deborah might feel threatened. In this case, her ego may instigate fault-finding. She might criticize the new colleague's lack of experience, her naivety about company culture, or her overly casual approach to senior staff. This judgment isn't about the new colleague, but about Deborah's ego trying to maintain its self-worth and sense of superiority.

Take another example of a man named John, an active member of his local fitness club. One day, a new, significantly fitter and stronger member joins the club. John's ego springs into action, comparing his fitness levels, muscle tone, and strength with this new entrant. When John's ego finds his physique lacking in comparison, it starts looking for faults in the new member to level the playing field. Perhaps he is too consumed with his looks, he's not friendly, or he doesn't respect the club's unspoken rules.

This exact mechanism plays out in countless scenarios— while shopping, on social media, at social gatherings, and even within families. Our ego is constantly engaged in this dance of comparison and judgment.

Here's another example. Mary, a diligent, ambitious young woman, graduated with a master's in business administration. Her hard work and perseverance paid off, and she landed a prestigious position at a top-tier consulting firm. With this role comes a title she had been striving for: Senior Consultant.

She first introduced herself with her new title at a business-community gathering. "Hello, I'm Mary, a Senior Consultant at XYC Consulting," she said with an undertone of pride. The sense of prestige that came with the title was intoxicating. She noticed that people's demeanors toward her subtly shifted as they acknowledged her title—a nod of respect here, a complimentary remark there. It felt like her title had validated her worth and the hard work she put in to get there.

Over time, Mary used her title more and more, not just in professional settings but in social ones. At parties, on social media bios, and even when meeting new people informally, she would ask people about their occupation. This approach provided her with an opening to casually introduce herself as "Senior Consultant at XYC Consulting."

Mary's title became integral to her identity—one she clung to firmly. It wasn't just about the job or role anymore. It had become a marker of her achievements, dedication, and intelligence. She would often engage in conversations about her job and subtly include comments about the high-profile projects she was leading or the significant impact her consultancy was making.

This constant referencing of her title and accomplishment seemed to enhance her self-worth and self-image. It made her feel distinguished, unique, and superior to others in a concrete way. It had become a source of egoic enhancement, a constant validation that she was more than just "Mary." She was Mary, the Senior Consultant.

However, this need to constantly reaffirm her title also created internal pressure. Any potential threat to her title or position, be it a challenging project or a talented recruit, caused her significant stress and anxiety. She realized she was heavily invested in this self-image, and any disruption threatened her very identity.

Her attachment to her title was a clear example of the ego's need to enhance its sense of self through identification with external content—in Mary's case, a prestigious job title. It served to boost her self-image, but, at the same time, it made her susceptible to constant comparisons with others, fear of failure, and stress. The experience highlighted the complex dynamics of the ego and its continual search for validation and enhancement.

The Role of the Victim

Unseen and unacknowledged, the ego can easily forge another self-image: the victim. Born from feelings of inadequacy and failure, this identity is bolstered by often unspoken self-talk, such as, "Nobody understands my pain. I've suffered more. I'm the ultimate martyr." This mindset transforms our defeats into a twisted badge of honor, further bolstering the ego's illusion of victimhood.

Complaining becomes the ego's weapon of choice to fortify this role. We lament our circumstances, companions, and the trivial frustrations of our daily lives. Every inconvenience morphs into an enemy, an assault on our victim identity. As the ego perceives threat after threat, we start to indulge in a constant stream of complaints, even about the most inconsequential issues.

Imagine yourself lounging in your backyard, basking in tranquility with this book. Out of nowhere, your neighbor's children organize a noisy pool party with booming hip-hop music. Your ego responds, "Every time I find some peace, these kids ruin it. I knew this would happen. Their parents should control them better. This isn't fair to me."

This irritation transforms the parents and their kids into your adversaries, fortifying your feeling of alienation from them. Suddenly, you're a victim, and they're your enemies, fueling a cycle of complaints to friends and family. Each time you see them, your disgust grows. You search for further proof of their shortcomings to reinforce your narrative of being a victim of inconsiderate neighbors.

Imagine another simple scenario: You're served a cold, unappetizing meal at a restaurant while other guests relish warm, generous portions. The ego interprets this minor setback as a personal offense, casting the waiter as a villain. In response, you may voice a complaint to soothe your bruised ego and assert your dominance: "Why would you serve me a cold meal? This is the second time this has happened." Alternatively, you may brood silently, nursing a grudge that leaves your companions puzzled about your mood. Such interactions fortify the ego's persona as a victim, amplifying a sense of moral superiority that validates our self-esteem.

Unaware of our innermost essence, we often slip into the role of the victim, painting ourselves as heroes wronged by the world. These examples show how easily the ego finds grievances in trivial situations, turning minor inconveniences into perceived injustices. Our complaints morph into a pathway to vindication, a vocal rebellion against these imagined slights. Yet this victim mentality keeps us bound to discontent, disconnected from the peace and joy of our true nature.

Of course, I'm not advocating for a martyr's passivity in the face of injustice—another ego ploy to play the victim. Victims of abuse, for instance, should not tolerate or justify mistreatment. Sometimes, the highest act of love might be to walk away and report the offender to prevent further harm.

Likewise, an amicable approach would suffice with the cold meal: "Sir? My meal is too cold for me to enjoy. Is it possible to have it reheated or replaced?" A polite, open-hearted demeanor keeps the ego at bay, fostering a connection with the waiter rather than building animosity.

Gratitude serves as a powerful countermeasure to the ego's tendency to adopt a victim mentality. It encourages acceptance of the present moment and nurtures inner peace. While complaining perpetuates a state of discontent, feeding into the ego's narrative of victimhood and misery, gratitude keeps us anchored in contentment. This mindset prevents the ego from undermining our happiness, thereby setting the stage for more positive and rewarding experiences.

Living Beyond the Ego: Insights from Paul's Teachings

As we've explored, many spiritual traditions contrast the ego with "being" or "consciousness." For example, Buddhism distinguishes the ego from *anatta*, or non-self. Similar ideas can be found in Hinduism, Taoism, Sufism, and Judaism. Understanding these contrasting states of the human experience is key to breaking down the barriers created by the ego.

With this in mind, I want to introduce a New Testament concept written by Paul that sheds light on this topic. While this study is somewhat theological, it offers valuable insights, particularly because it's not widely recognized in modern Christian circles.

As we will see, Paul, a central figure in the New Testament, offers profound insights into transcending the ego and awakening to our higher, true self. Although his words were tailored to his specific audience and culture, they resonate deeply with the teachings of other spiritual traditions that position the ego in opposition to being. Paul writes, "I have been crucified with Christ; nevertheless I (*zaō*) live, yet not I (ego), but Christ lives in me, and the life which I (*zaō*) now live in the flesh."[3]

Here, Paul distinguishes between two forms of "I" in the original Greek. The first "I" refers to the ego, which no longer lives. The second "I," *zaō*, signifies *aliveness, breath, life, or being*—a concept parallel to today's understanding of consciousness.

Remarkably, Paul makes a connection between this consciousness—"I" or *zaō*—and Christ. In Greek, "Christ" functions not as a noun but as an adjective, which describes or adds detail to a noun, highlighting qualities, characteristics, or other attributes. So, when Paul speaks about the nature of *zaō*—or consciousness—he identifies its defining characteristic as Christ, a term meaning "anointed."

Of course, Jesus was called Christ. In other words, "Christ" was used to describe the anointed state of being that Jesus embodied. The question then arises: Why was Jesus called Christ? According to many within the Christian tradition, it is because Jesus embodied a unity of self that was inseparable from God. His perception of "self" extended beyond individuality to include all of life, even those marginalized by society. Paul hints at this understanding of Christ in his writings when he speaks of Christ as the center of all things, in whom all things exist and have their being.

Therefore, when Paul links the *zaō*-self with Christ, he refers to a profound internal awareness of our deepest self —Christ, an anointed state of being where we identify with the transcendent loving Presence that undergirds all reality. God is in us, and we are in God. Since God is the innermost essence of all things, Paul identifies with this essence as his true self.

To illustrate his awakening, Paul uses vivid language, describing the ego-self as crucified—enduring intense suffering until death. For Paul, death wasn't about annihilation or ceasing to exist, but about separation. He believed that when a person dies physically, the spirit continues to live on in a spiritual realm, simply separated from the body. In the text we are exploring, Paul refers to this sense of separation when he speaks of a different kind of death —a "death before physical death"—where the ego separates from the state of pure being, creating a gap between the ego-self and Christ-consciousness, or the true self.

Paul describes experiencing this separation from the narrow, personalized ego when he explains that he now lives from Christ-consciousness. In this state, he is aware of his eternal—or, more accurately, timeless—nature, existing outside the confines of time in the ever-present now. This is a state where Paul experienced unity with God and all creation. In other words, he became "born again," as discussed in the last chapter—a state free from mental labels and judgments, rooted in the present moment, where he experienced the world through a consciousness of unity and love.

Paul's identification with Christ-consciousness doesn't erase the role of the ego in recognizing physical separateness in the world. Instead, he seems to propose that he is no longer lost in the mental story of who he is, based on his personality and physical form. Instead, he has become aware of his true identity as pure, unconditioned consciousness in unity with the One-Life—God.

We could describe this shift as an awakening. Paul has awakened from the illusion of separation that is tied to the physical world and become aware of a deeper, more unifying dimension of oneness. From this "Christ" dimension, a wellspring of peace, love, and wisdom flow into the physical world.

Have you ever felt trapped by the stories you tell yourself about who you are? Paul's journey suggests that there is a deeper identity waiting to be discovered—a self that is connected to something much greater. Although the ego-self still played a role in navigating daily life, Paul is now aware of a deeper reality within. He no longer sees the ego-self as his true identity. Instead, he has awakened to Christ-consciousness, where Christ is all and in all. There is a clear separation between his ego-identity and his true self as Christ-consciousness. Paul is no longer lost in the mental narrative about who he is but has awakened to his true essence, observing his thoughts and emotions as fleeting and distant from his true self.

Paul describes this experience using the imagery of crucifixion and resurrection. The ego-self, which had been developed since childhood, has been crucified. In its place, a new person has emerged—one that is fully aware of its union with God and all creation.

From Ego to Essence: Embracing the Stillness Within

What can we learn from this theological discussion? When we awaken to our true essence, we perceive egoic thoughts as separate from our true self. We no longer identify with these thoughts, realizing they are not who we truly are. Initially, this awakening might create only a small gap between our awareness of the true self as consciousness and the constant stream of thoughts that invade our minds. However, through cultivating inner stillness, we can expand this gap.

Inner stillness allows us to silence the mind's obsession with the past and future, bringing us into the present moment, where our deepest essence resides. As we deepen our awareness of this stillness, the separation between our true self and the egoic thoughts becomes more pronounced. We start to see these thoughts for what they are—temporary, fleeting, and often rooted in fear or desire—rather than as defining aspects of who we are. This creates a decisive shift in how we experience life, enabling us to live from a place of peace, unity, and love rather than being driven by the restless mind.

Through inner stillness, we awaken to our true self, which is always present in the now. In this state, we experience the world with clarity and compassion, free from the mental labels and judgments that once clouded our perception. The psalmist's words, "Be still, and know that I am God,"[4] resonate deeply with this awareness. They remind us that in the stillness of our being, we find not only our true self but also our connection to God, where the illusion of separation dissolves, and we come to know the divine essence within us—the very "Christ in us"[5] that Paul speaks of—as the ultimate essence of who we are.

7

LIGHT ON SHADOWS

Within each of us lies a hidden world, an uncharted terrain of buried experiences and suppressed emotions. This secret realm lurks beneath the surface of our cognitive mind, yet its presence is deeply felt, quietly shaping the course of our lives in ways we often don't realize.

These inner shadows hold the power to stir something within us—a sudden flash of anger, an unexpected wave of sadness. They're the unseen forces that can fuel anxiety, stir up self-doubt, or cloud our joy. Though they operate in the background, they leave their mark on our thoughts, feelings, and actions, reminding us that what we bury doesn't disappear.

For example, have you ever wondered why someone's casual comment or simple action can stir up a whirlwind of anger within you? Do you wonder what invisible shadow within your subconscious is setting off such volatile reactions, or what deeply seated memory is responsible for that unexpected surge of sorrow?

We often find ourselves at odds with these shadows, as they don't represent our best selves. We long to rise above these internal battles, to break free from these inner "demons" that keep us shackled to our past and prevent us from manifesting the reality we desire.

When referring to our "inner shadows," I mean the unconscious aspects of our personalities that we may not be fully aware of. These include suppressed emotions, subconscious fears, past traumas, or unexpressed desires. Essentially, they are parts of ourselves that we might not acknowledge or often hide from our conscious awareness.

These shadows are often formed from early life experiences. For instance, if we undergo a painful event as a child, our brain might "store" this memory away as a means of protection, so we are prepared to put our guard up if we encounter a similar set of circumstances. However, while this memory is hidden from our conscious mind, it still influences our behaviors, beliefs, and reactions in the present. It's as if these past experiences cast a shadow on our present actions.

The shadows can also come to light in our reactions to others. We may react strongly to a trait in someone else because it mirrors a part of ourselves that we don't want to accept. Have you ever reacted unusually strongly to someone else's specific characteristics or behaviors? This could be a sign that you're coming face to face with your inner shadow.

Often, what annoys us about others is actually something that's lying dormant within us, something we're trying to suppress or deny. This can happen with traits that we find undesirable or unappealing. For instance, we might find ourselves intensely irritated by someone's constant need for approval, only to realize that deep down, we also crave validation from others.

Similarly, this could happen with traits we admire but believe we lack. Feeling envious or insecure around someone who is confidently expressing their ideas could reflect our own unacknowledged desire to be more assertive and outspoken.

This phenomenon is often referred to as "mirroring" in psychology. It's like our subconscious is holding up a mirror, showing us the parts of ourselves that we've hidden away or refused to acknowledge.

How Shadows Are Formed

When we're truly present—in the "now"—our consciousness is free from the mind's fixation on our surroundings, the body, and time. As we discovered already, in that transcended state, all potentialities exist simultaneously in the quantum field and, once observed, can emerge out of their state of potentiality, causing what physicists refer to as a "collapse of the wave function."

To frame this in the words of Jesus again, all things are possible through faith. Here, faith is an inner state of peace, a coherence between the "heart, soul, mind, and body" that allows us to perceive and enter what Jesus called the kingdom of God—a realm of limitless possibilities. This state of being is characterized by an awareness of a presence filled with awe and love, profoundly influencing how we perceive reality. It's from this state that creativity is enhanced, tapping into the universal divine mind.

However, most of us struggle to sustain this state of presence and inner stillness. Our thoughts seem to occur automatically—they're involuntary, repetitive, and possess a life of their own. We find ourselves at the mercy of an internal voice that is heavily influenced by our past and perpetually seeks to reenact it, regardless of our conscious desires. It's as if it's echoing the shadows of our subconscious.

So, how are these subconscious shadows formed? When we have an experience that triggers a strong emotional reaction, our brain's limbic system springs into action, initiating a chemical release that transmits the emotion from the experience into our heart and, subsequently, our entire body. As soon as these messages reach our body, the body resonates with the emotion, producing a corresponding sensation.

Our body then promptly mirrors these feelings back to our brain, triggering a thought about the experience.

This process establishes a feedback loop where a thought about a past incident heightens the body's sensation, amplifying the original thought. If this loop of thinking and feeling about the event recurs long enough, it can become habitual. With enough repetition, the experience, the thoughts, and the emotions merge into a single *memorized emotion.*[1] This ingrained pattern then defines a state of being, establishing a consistent way of feeling and thinking about ourselves and our world.

Initially, this mind-body loop might only lead to transient moods. We might have a negative thought, which creates an unpleasant feeling in our body, prompting additional thoughts that reinforce the original negativity. This process can influence our mood. In other words, something in our environment could trigger this loop, causing us to experience temporary emotional disturbances.

For instance, let's consider a scenario where you had a tough day at work. Your boss criticized your project in front of your colleagues. This experience generates a strong emotional response, and your limbic system responds by sending out a cascade of chemicals that produce a feeling of humiliation and inadequacy in your body.

When you get home, these feelings still linger. Your body, resonating with these emotions, mirrors them back to your brain, causing you to think about the incident again. This renews the feelings of humiliation, thereby creating a feedback loop. You're now locked in this loop of negative thoughts and emotions.

Suddenly, a family member makes an innocuous comment about a small mistake you made—perhaps you forgot to buy something from the grocery store. Ordinarily, this wouldn't bother you, but you react strongly because you're still caught up in the feedback loop from earlier. You feel a surge of anger and respond harshly.

Over time, these negative moods might become more than just temporary states. If allowed to persist, they can become ingrained in your subconscious and emerge as part of your personality, influencing how you perceive yourself and interact with the world around you. Thus, a thought can eventually mold your identity, shaping the lens through which you view and respond to your reality.

For instance, let's assume that whenever your boss criticizes your work, or you make a minor mistake at home, you repeatedly fall into this negative mind-body loop. The feelings of humiliation and inadequacy triggered by your boss or the frustration prompted by your home situation begin to carve a deep groove in your subconscious. Before you know it, you've associated criticism and mistakes with these intense negative emotions. You start to anticipate humiliation and frustration in similar scenarios, even before they occur.

This anticipation, a form of anxiety, only serves to strengthen the mind-body loop. Now, you're not just reacting to specific incidents—you're anticipating them, and your anticipation triggers the same emotional response. This pattern turns into a self-fulfilling prophecy. You expect to feel humiliated and frustrated, and so you do.

Thus, an initial fleeting thought has become a defining aspect of your personality. This mind-body feedback loop has significantly shaped your self-image and behavior, demonstrating the emotions' influential role in molding our identities and realities.

Who Controls Who?

Once a specific pattern of thought and feeling becomes ingrained, it operates automatically. Let's take the example of a woman who was left by her partner, transforming her life overnight into that of a single mother. The way her partner left was deeply hurtful, and for a prolonged period, she was consumed with thoughts about the injustices she endured. These thoughts stirred powerful emotions, creating a feedback loop of hurt and victimhood.

Fast forward twenty-five years. The details of the incident no longer need to be consciously thought about for the feeling of victimization to surface. Her life experiences are seen through a filter of victimhood, suffering, and unhappiness. Her body has adapted to this emotional state. It has become her new norm.

Research suggests that by the time we reach our thirties, our personality—our sense of self—is fully formed. Our reactions, attitudes, behaviors, skills, beliefs, and perceptions about reality have been subconsciously programmed into us.[2] This programming guides our lives, steering us along paths of habitual thought and action.

Consequently, we find ourselves repeatedly thinking the same thoughts, experiencing the same feelings, and reacting similarly to various situations. Our views about faith, politics, and societal norms become fixed.

While these fixed viewpoints might limit our ability to perceive reality from different angles, this established programming offers numerous practical advantages. It enables us to perform routine tasks without conscious thought, freeing our minds to focus on other things.

For instance, because we have habituated the process of brushing our teeth or driving a car, we don't need to consciously think about each step involved in these activities every time we do them. Instead, our subconscious programming takes over, guiding us through these tasks efficiently and effectively. This allows us to focus our conscious attention on other tasks or thoughts.

Similarly, our fixed beliefs and perceptions can serve as a helpful compass, guiding us through the complexities of life. They help us make sense of the world, providing a stable foundation from which to understand and respond to our experiences. For instance, if we've grown up with a strong sense of compassion and empathy, these qualities become part of our subconscious programming and influ-ence our interactions with others. We might instinctively respond with kindness and understanding in situations where others might react differently.

However, the same programming can also lead us down less beneficial paths. It might lead us to overeat when stressed, judge our friends when we feel offended, or grumble about our lives when things don't go as planned. We might blame our loved ones for our problems or use our past as an excuse for chronic unhappiness. This auto-matic response system often shapes our lives in ways we don't consciously realize.

How Early Childhood Impacts Us as Adults

Often, experiences that imprint emotional memories on us as adults have a diminished impact because we can use our prefrontal cortex, the region responsible for complex cognitive behavior, personality expression, and decision-making, to analyze and logically introspect on what happened. Over time, we can reflect on an experience and lessen its impact on our lives.

However, our brains are not fully developed until we reach our twenties. Therefore, the earlier the experience occurs, the greater its potential to cause problems later in life. For instance, a newborn baby's cortex is not yet fully developed. As a result, explicit memories, which are conscious and intentionally recalled, don't form during infancy. This means we don't have direct access to recollections of experiences from our earliest couple years of life via the prefrontal cortex.

However, this does not mean that our experiences during this time leave no trace on our brain, body, heart, and later life. Quite the contrary, in fact. Our early experiences, particularly those involving our primary caregivers, leave an indelible imprint, not as explicit memories but as implicit ones, also known as "feeling" memories. These memories are stored in the lower parts of our brain, the limbic system, and the cerebellum—our brain's "automatic pilot"—where routines are stored and executed without conscious thought.[3]

Implicit memories are typically emotional and visceral, and they shape our perceptions and responses at this subconscious level. For instance, if we experienced consistent unrest, deregulation, or disconnection from a primary caregiver during infancy, this could lead to feelings of insecurity and distress. While we may not have explicit memories of these experiences, they become part of our implicit memory, influencing how we perceive and interpret reality as we age.

Such experiences can shape our attachment style, which is our typical way of interacting in close relationships. If our early experiences involved insecurity and disconnection, we might develop an insecure attachment style, manifesting in excessive anxiety in relationships, fear of abandonment, or difficulty trusting others.

In essence, our earliest experiences, although not remembered in the conventional sense, are crucial in shaping our perceptions, behaviors, and interpretations of reality throughout life. These implicit memories influence our emotional landscape and interpersonal dynamics in profound ways.

For example, consider Sophia, a woman in her early thirties, known for her vivacious spirit and infectious laughter. But beneath her sparkling exterior lies a tangle of insecurities that confounds even her closest friends.

From the time Sophia was a baby, her mother, a struggling single parent, was often overwhelmed by her circumstances. The stress of her situation seeped into her relationship with Sophia, leading to sporadic episodes of unrest, deregulation, and disconnection. While Sophia's mother did her best, the inconsistency in her caregiving left its mark on Sophia.

Sophia's prefrontal cortex was not yet developed enough as a newborn to form explicit memories of these challenging experiences. She holds no recollection of those nights when her mother, burdened by anxiety, couldn't spare the time for soothing lullabies or comforting smiles due to sheer exhaustion.

However, the lower parts of her brain encoded these experiences, not as explicit memories but as implicit, feeling memories. While Sophia doesn't consciously remember her mother's anxiety and emotional inconsistency, they have imprinted themselves into her emotional responses and behavior patterns.

Now an accomplished professional, Sophia often finds herself wracked with inexplicable insecurities. Her relationships undergo a rollercoaster of emotions, marked by an intense fear of abandonment. She battles a constant need for validation from her partners, friends, and colleagues, an invisible thread connecting her present with her past.

Despite her lack of explicit infancy memories, the feeling memories embedded in Sophia's brain have shaped her perceptions and interpretations of reality. They manifest as an underlying anxiety in her relationships and a deeply entrenched fear of not being good enough.

Sophia's story is a vivid testament to how our earliest experiences, even those we cannot consciously recall, profoundly shape our emotional world. It underscores the power of feeling memories and their lasting influence on our perception of reality.

Despite our yearnings for a better life and the desire to allow our true self—our consciousness—to guide us, we often find ourselves trapped by our past. We may think our rational mind is in the driver's seat, but the reality is quite different. Our thoughts are shaped by the feedback loop between our heart and brain that has formed our personality and now controls our lives. This is why change can feel so challenging.

We often find ourselves caught in a seemingly endless cycle of habitual thoughts and emotions. No matter how much our mind attempts to break free from this cycle, it finds itself bound. When the mind tries to escape, the body can fall into a state of chaos, triggering distress signals and even health-related issues.

You see, our body has become accustomed to certain feelings, and when we attempt to disrupt these habitual patterns, it resists. The mind immediately generates a barrage of reasons for why change isn't possible. It's as though our own minds become our greatest obstacle to change, trapping us in patterns of thought and behavior that no longer serve us.

Recreating Our Past

Ultimately, this habitual pattern traps us in a cycle of recreating the past, making us resistant to change. We become addicted to the familiar feelings that our history evokes, and, despite our best intentions to improve our lives, we continue manifesting the reality we've always known.

Consider the example of a young woman who has been seeking a romantic partner but whose father was verbally or physically abusive toward her. These deep-seated memories, embedded in her limbic system or mid-brain, influence her self-perception and sense of worth.

Meanwhile, her cerebellum—the lower part of the brain —has stored patterns of defensive behaviors and automatic responses that she used to cope with the abuse as a child, such as avoidance, emotional shutdown, or even aggressiveness. With time and repetition, these reactions became ingrained in the cerebellum and are triggered automatically whenever she encounters situations reminiscent of the abuse.

Her prefrontal cortex, responsible for reasoning and decision-making, continually attempts to make sense of these experiences. However, chronic abuse can cause overwhelming emotional responses from the limbic system, impairing the prefrontal cortex's ability to think clearly and make rational decisions. This dysfunction may lead to a perpetual state of hypervigilance, anxiety, and cognitive impairment.

As this child grew into adulthood, the deeply ingrained patterns would have persisted. She might find herself reacting irrationally or excessively, as her cerebellum continues to trigger defensive behaviors learned in childhood. Emotional responses that were adaptive in the abusive environment can become maladaptive elsewhere, resulting in relationship problems, stress-management difficulties, and self-esteem struggles.

Even her thoughts and beliefs about herself, processed in the prefrontal cortex, may be profoundly impacted. She might have internalized messages of worthlessness or fear from her abusive father, which now influence her self-perception and worldview. She may unconsciously seek a "healer" partner or find herself drawn to destructive and abusive partners because they feel familiar. While she doesn't understand why, her subconscious convinces her that this is what she deserves or how she will be cared for.

To outsiders, her tendency to choose abusive relationships is baffling and illogical. She cannot even consciously comprehend her choices. However, she continues to recreate her past due to the programming in her mid and lower brain, where 95 percent of all brain activity occurs.

Her situation is not unique. We are all products of our unconscious memories, often reenacting our pasts. Our inner shadows influence our perception of reality and life experience, trapping us in familiar patterns and perpetuating suffering.

But can we transcend this inner suffering? Can we illuminate the shadows within and attain inner wholeness? As unconventional as it may seem, the union of timeless wisdom from Jesus and the groundbreaking insights of neurocardiology might hold the key.

As we will explore, this intricate interplay between spiritual teachings and scientific revelations is more than theory and dogma. It presents a practical guide to dispelling our shadows and immersing ourselves in a profound state of wholeness.

Freedom

One day during Jesus's travels, the religious leaders, in an attempt to trap him, presented him with a woman charged with adultery. Despite the contempt and shame heaped upon her by these authorities, Jesus responded with nonjudgment. His compassion and forgiveness toward someone whom these leaders considered the embodiment of sin amazed many of his followers. As whispers and reactions swirled around, Jesus turned to his followers and declared, "You shall know the truth, and the truth will set you free."[4]

Implied in his words is the idea that they were not free. It's no wonder that this struck a chord of indignation in many of them. In their eyes, they were liberated. Their people hadn't been enslaved for centuries. What, then, was Jesus implying when he suggested they needed to know the truth in order to be free—people who indeed felt they were already on the path of righteousness as believers and followers of Jesus?

This is when Jesus broached the topic of sin. For context, in the eyes of these believers, the adulterous woman was the embodiment of sin. This situation is not unlike today, where many religions, perhaps especially certain groups within Christianity, equate sin with societal and moral degradation, violations of divine laws, or behaviors they deem unethical. But Jesus pointed to a more profound and nuanced understanding of sin that transcended traditional religious interpretations.

A more accurate understanding of sin is the condition of "missing the mark" of our true identity. Several factors support this interpretation. First, the word "sin" is a noun referring to a thing, person, or, in this case, a state of being. Secondly, "sin" literally means "to miss the mark," as if we were aiming an arrow at a target and shot wide. Therefore, a more fitting interpretation of sin would be a state of being in which an individual has lost touch with the essence of who they truly are, rather than a specific act of moral wrongdoing. The selfish behaviors typically associated with sin merely reflect this disconnection from our true self—the unconditioned consciousness, where the heart resonates with love and peace and a profound sense of interconnectedness with all things.

So, what blinds us to knowing ourselves as consciousness —our true self? The shadows or internal darkness we harbor. How do these inner shadows take root? In the ancient Hebrew culture, the respected prophet and poet Jeremiah posited that the heart's nature is deceptive, so much so that even our rational mind is often oblivious to its true intentions. The ancient text suggests our hearts bear scars akin to footprints. Jeremiah's words hint that external influences have cast these shadows, preventing our intrinsic light of consciousness from shining through our hearts.[5]

Past emotional wounds have subtly but deeply impacted us. Whether we were made to feel lesser by others or faced demeaning remarks that chipped away at our self-worth, the resultant scars have rendered us vulnerable and fragile, as Jeremiah noted. In this context, many people find themselves in a state of "sin," as Jesus described it.

So, when we look at the depth of what Jesus suggested, he essentially said that the real problem was not in our actions, such as adultery, but in what happened to us to get to that point. How did our hearts become so broken that we found ourselves in these predicaments? What internal shadows have led us down a trajectory dominated by negative emotions and thoughts, to the point where our actions only amplify our inner suffering?

Heart Coherence

Research conducted by the HeartMath Institute, a recognized science-focused organization, offers profound insights into the complex interplay between heart activity and our thoughts and behaviors. Their findings reveal that emotions like love, appreciation, and care immediately impact the heart's rhythm, making it more "coherent."[6]

This coherence triggers a sequence of neural and biochemical events affecting almost every organ in our body. The heart rate decelerates, and the body's internal system relaxes, reducing wear and tear on nerves and internal organs. Additionally, HeartMath's research found that a "coherent heart" enhances mental clarity and intuition.[7] Participants who consistently experienced "coherence" due to positive feelings demonstrated better control over their perception, reducing stress and amplifying their effectiveness. Their interactions became character-ized by greater compassion and understanding, displaying an internal freedom that made them more altruistic and forgiving.

In contrast, negative emotions such as frustration, anxiety, and stress can cause an erratic, "incoherent" pattern in the heart's rhythms. Such "incoherent" patterns can result in many adverse health outcomes. They can spike cortisol levels, indicating stress; impair cognitive capabilities; increase vulnerability to chronic ailments; and weaken the immune system's defenses.

Over time, persistent incoherence can accelerate aging, reduce resilience, and elevate the risk of cardiovascular diseases. Furthermore, these erratic patterns can also influence our mental wellbeing, leading to heightened levels of anxiety, depression, and emotional fatigue and potentially fostering anger, bitterness, and a range of harmful behaviors.

This research reiterates the link between the heart and inner shadows and the impact of holistic wellbeing, a sentiment echoing the profound wisdom of Jesus.

The Truth Makes You Free

Revisiting Jesus's declaration, "You shall know the truth, and the truth will make you free," may provide us some added clarity. When Jesus spoke of freedom from sin, his focus was not on rectifying wrong actions but addressing the root problem—the shadows of our hearts. He aimed not merely to treat the symptoms but to understand and heal what caused them in the first place. His aim was holistic: comprehending what steered someone away from their true essence and uncovering the path leading back to that pristine state. Jesus sought to answer the question: How can we address our inner darkness and reshape our perspective to resonate with peace, love, and joy?

Jesus proposed that knowing the truth would make people free. But what is this truth, and how could they know it? The Aramaic term for "truth" Jesus employed is *shrara*, denoting an inner light or clarity within the heart.[8] An illuminated heart casts no shadows; it operates coherently. This state epitomizes inner peace, profound love, and gratitude, with consciousness anchored firmly in the present, undisturbed by past scars or embedded traumas.

Furthermore, the Aramaic perspective on "knowing the truth" is an ongoing awareness, not a singular epiphany. Truth, as inner heart luminance, ceaselessly guides our path. It symbolizes unfettered consciousness basking in the now. The act of knowing extends beyond mere intellectual acknowledgment. It envelops a profound realization that surpasses the cerebral, touching the realms of intuitive wisdom, beyond logic.

Envision "knowing the truth" as awareness of our core essence as pure consciousness, characterized by unwavering peace, boundless love, and a profound connection to all existence. This transcendental state harmonizes with the heart's coherence, supporting mental clarity and intuitive knowledge transcending mere intellectual constructs.

Meditate Within Your Heart

So, how can we practically apply these concepts to our inner shadows? Given that our emotional memories are deeply entrenched in our mid-brain, coupled with the automatic responses from our primal brain, how do we navigate when old patterns resurface? How do we seamlessly incorporate these principles, ensuring we neutralize the habitual emotional reactions that arise?

As you probably guessed, the answer lies in achieving a state of inner heart coherence, an elevated state characterized by peace and love. This state can recalibrate the long-standing neurological pathways in our emotional brain. The pressing question then becomes: How can we practically nurture this heart coherence, granting us access to address deeply rooted emotional memories?

The ancient wisdom of the psalmist David offered us a clue when he wrote that meditation was the way to commune with the heart.[9] While modern interpretations of meditation owe much to Eastern philosophies, its deep roots within Jesus's cultural context often go overlooked. The Bible references meditation over twenty times, with many more indirect nods to the practice. For instance,

Paul's words about the "eyes of the heart"[10] being enlightened intimate a deep connection to heart coherence.

More recent scientific findings reveal the heart's astounding intelligence. It boasts over 40,000 neurons that interface with the brain and the body. The benefits of meditation are numerous. For example, it can foster organized heart patterns, leading to heart coherence. The resulting benefits are manifold: decreased heart rate, lower blood pressure, and an uptick in parasympathetic activity, which conserves energy, slows the heart rate, and stimulates glandular activity. Evidence also suggests that meditation amplifiès heart-rate variability, a sign of enhanced emotional equilibrium and cardiovascular health. It can also reduce stress hormone production, boost blood flow, and expedite post-stress recovery, mitigating heart disease risk factors.[11]

Yet, the effects of meditation aren't confined to the heart. Groundbreaking studies detail significant neurological transformations. These include diminished amygdala activity (responsible for anxiety and fear), restricted access to past emotional pain in the hippocampus, and augmented brain-stem activity, enhancing the brain's communication with the body and fortifying the immune system.[12] Furthermore, neuroscientists link meditation to improved emotional wellness, communication prowess, problem-solving skills, and creativity. This suggests the brain, far from being fixed, dynamically evolves through heartfelt meditation.

So, when we find ourselves wrestling with recurring negative emotions, thoughts, or behaviors, meditation acts as a
conduit to our hearts, heightening our awareness of our
true self as pure consciousness. This amplified self-awareness fosters a sense of detachment, delineating our true
self—our core consciousness—from the sudden surges of
anger, jealousy, and rage that often emerge during
stressful moments. It shines the light of consciousness on
emotions steeped with anxiety, shame, and guilt, creating
separation between our transient feelings and our
unchanging essence, effectively neutralizing and
tempering the intensity of these emotions.

Putting Meditation into Practice

The first step in meditation is to find inner stillness,
attuned with the kingdom of God, as explored in Chapter
5. This internal state of peace creates heart coherence,
sending waves of calm throughout the body, setting the
stage for deep-seated love and forgiveness to mend
bygone traumas.

Jesus emphasized this when he alluded to the transformative power of the truth that sets us free. He suggested that
"abiding" in his word, or *logos* in Greek, as mentioned in
Chapter 4, would usher us into a renewed state of existence, enabling awareness of this emancipating truth.
Here, "abide" transcends its superficial meaning, urging us
to immerse ourselves wholly in the present moment. This
logos represents a conscious observer that, while tran-

scending matter, space, and time, simultaneously permeates it, offering an eternal, unchanging foundation for all of life's experiences.

In essence, to dwell in the word is to be profoundly present, acknowledging our core consciousness and establishing a connection to an inner reservoir of peace, love, and wisdom. At this juncture, we communicate with our hearts, allowing the radiant consciousness to shine upon our internal shadows. Freedom emerges when the complex issues embedded in our subconscious yield to the light of consciousness because our hearts are in a state of coherence.

When we are ensnared by negative emotions and maladaptive reflexes, the solution lies in conscious acknowledgment. Shine the light of consciousness on these feelings, pause, and cultivate heart coherence until the innate guiding light dispels these shadows. Subsequent chapters will explore specific meditative techniques that have empowered many to experience such inner freedom.

Light on Shadows

So, what is the critical point to remember from this chapter? In the intricate, myriad moments of our existence, the dance between light and shadow plays an enduring role. By returning to the place of inner stillness and the light of awareness, we begin to illuminate the dark corners of our soul, bringing into focus what was previously hidden. Our endeavor to understand and meditate within our hearts is a transformative journey that has the potential to bring about deep-rooted healing and heart coherence.

In the next chapter, we will delve into inner hidden spiritual, psychological, and social maps that subtly guide the path our lives take. Imagine these maps as the foundational operating system shaping our perception of reality. Just as any software requires an optimal operating system, so does our life. The ultimate goal is to navigate by a map that steers us toward inner wellbeing and a brighter, more harmonious world for all.

8

NAVIGATING OUR INNER MAPS

H ave you ever wondered why your staunchly partisan neighbor passionately champions political views that seem alien to you or why your college friend, who hails from a different nationality, cherishes traditions that feel so unfamiliar? Why does a news story on racial issues resonate deeply with one person yet is dismissed by another? Why can two individuals have such varied interpretations of the same spiritual text?

Our perceptions of reality are as varied as fingerprints— distinct, complex, and molded by myriad influences. The families we are raised in, the media we consume, the company we keep, our religious affiliations and even our educational histories craft what can be termed our "inner maps." These maps, often constructed subconsciously, influence our navigation through the vast expanse of reality, resulting in the diverse interpretations and reactions we witness daily.

A compelling illustration of these inner maps can be found in a concept that has gained considerable traction in recent years: unconscious biases. These instantaneous judgments, born from our entrenched beliefs, cultural milieu, personal histories, and societal cues, play a pivotal role in how we interpret reality.

Unconscious biases act as mental shortcuts, automatically shaping our views, decisions, and behaviors without our conscious realization. They are the mind's method for quickly sorting and categorizing incoming information, relying on previous experiences and societal norms. Regardless of how open-minded individuals may believe themselves to be, everyone possesses these biases. For example, someone might unconsciously trust or distrust another person based on their facial features, accent, or name. These biases span various dimensions, including gender, race, education, and geographic origin.

Operating as selective filters, unconscious biases highlight information that confirms our pre-existing beliefs while often disregarding evidence to the contrary. This selective attention affects everything from professional choices to interpersonal interactions, potentially leading us to favor or exclude certain groups unwittingly. This reinforces existing stereotypes and contributes to the deepening of societal divides.

Central to understanding unconscious biases is recognizing the intricate unconscious frameworks that navigate our engagement with the world around us. Much like a computer's operating system, these maps are complex amalgamations of psychological, cognitive, and social frameworks that guide our thoughts, emotions, and actions.

A Glimpse into Inner Maps

Over the past century, intellectual trailblazers like Jean Piaget, Ken Wilber, and James Fowler have pioneered the exploration of human development, charting between four and nine stages of these inner maps.[1] Jean Piaget, for instance, introduced a theory outlining four pivotal stages of cognitive development, offering a window into the evolving human intellect. In contrast, Ken Wilber's Integral Theory provides a holistic view, categorizing the human experience across nine nuanced "stages of consciousness."

At first glance, the concept of these stages may appear to conflict with the idea of pure, unattached consciousness. However, Wilber resolves this apparent paradox by distinguishing between the *states* and *stages* of consciousness, highlighting their complementary roles in our inner evolution.

Wilber explains that our ultimate and true self is pure consciousness, often referred to as the "witness" or "nondual awareness." This awareness is not something external that we observe; rather, it is the timeless and spaceless ground of being—the very awareness observing all phenomena. It is ever-present, regardless of the stage of development or the content of experience.[2]

To further clarify: States of consciousness are temporary experiences that offer direct but fleeting glimpses of our true self. For instance, during deep meditation, mystical experiences, or altered states, we may temporarily experience nondual awareness or the witnessing state, recognizing that our true nature is the consciousness that observes all mental and physical phenomena. These state experiences can occur at any stage of development, but they are often only fully integrated or understood once we reach higher stages of consciousness.[3] The key is to stabilize these temporary states into a permanent realization by integrating them into daily life, a process that typically unfolds as we progress through the stages of consciousness.

On the other hand, stages of consciousness represent the developmental process through which we gradually become aware of consciousness as our true self. As we advance, there is a gradual disidentification from these limited aspects, culminating in the realization that our true self is not tied to any particular form or stage. Instead, it is the awareness that transcends and includes all stages.

Wilber emphasizes that while states can occur spontaneously, stages unfold progressively, each building on the previous one. Fully integrating state experiences into a stable realization typically requires advancing through higher stages of consciousness.

This understanding illuminates the path of human development and societal evolution. For simplicity, I will refer to these stages using terms such as *egocentric* (me-focused), *ethnocentric* (we-focused), and *world-centric* (everyone-focused), with the ultimate trajectory moving toward a *Christ-centric* or *Kosmic-centric* (universal unity) stage.

Before diving deeper into each phase of these inner maps, it's crucial to note a few considerations regarding these stages of perspective:

Gradual Transition: These stages often overlap, gradually making the transition from one to the next. We don't instantly jump from one altitude to the next but progress through intermediary phases, each offering a broader view of life. However, once firmly rooted in a particular stage, it becomes challenging to revert to a narrower, less inclusive stage of consciousness.

Nonjudgmental Framework: Outlining these stages isn't an exercise in labeling or judging others. Ultimately, judging others or viewing some people as less or greater than ourselves is rooted in ego. Instead, the purpose of sharing these stages of consciousness is threefold:

- *Personal Insight:* Understanding these stages can clarify our journey and catalyze personal growth.

- *Healthier Relationships:* Recognizing these stages aids us in better understanding and empathizing with loved ones, fostering deeper connections and mutual respect.
- *Broader Societal Understanding:* This framework offers a lens to discern societal differences and dynamics, from political divisions to cultural disparities. By grasping these underlying structures, we can foster greater compassion, understanding, and effective communication across varied stages of consciousness.

Egocentrism: The "Me" Stage

At birth, we lack a distinct sense of self. The boundaries between our internal and external worlds are blurred; everything seems unified. We don't yet grasp the concept of our own body in relation to the surrounding environment.

But, as weeks turn into months, this nascent consciousness begins to evolve. A budding awareness of "self" and "other" emerges, and by around eighteen months, a more defined sense of identity takes shape. At this stage, the notions of "I," "me," and "mine" come into play, intertwined with inherent desires for security, safety, and affirmation.

This phase is known as the egocentric or "me" stage. Here, the ego takes center stage. As young children, we're primarily driven by our needs and wants, which are crucial in building our sense of self. However, for some of us, difficult experiences like trauma, a lack of affection, or the absence of positive role models can cause us to remain stuck in this self-centered stage even as we grow older.

When this happens, our world remains focused on our feelings, needs, and perspectives. It becomes challenging to see things from someone else's point of view, and we might start to believe that our way of seeing the world is the only way. This mindset can make it difficult to understand or empathize with others, leading to a perspective where what's right for us overshadows everything else. In extreme cases, this self-centeredness can manifest as narcissism, where empathy is lacking, and our actions may become harmful to ourselves and others.

Even in this "me" stage, we might have moments of deep connection to God or something greater than ourselves—a sense of unity, profound love, or the presence of something sacred. However, when we're stuck in a "me" mindset, these experiences can quickly become tools to boost our ego rather than growth opportunities. We might start to see God as something that exists to serve our needs, and our spiritual practices may become more about getting what we want than genuinely connecting with the divine.

In this stage, God is often perceived as a magical entity primarily serving and elevating us. Spiritual experiences are leveraged to bolster our ego, showcasing us as especially "chosen" or "blessed." Worship and prayer can become transactional acts to win God's favor and blessings.

Despite the limitations of this inner map, interactions with God at this stage can still be genuine. However, due to the constraints of the egocentric perspective, these experiences often take on a self-centered hue, reinforcing the ego rather than fostering actual spiritual growth.

Fortunately, human development continues. As we evolve, our perspective broadens, leading us to more inclusive, compassionate, and selfless stages of consciousness. Each transition offers a more elevated viewpoint, transforming how we see, interpret, and engage with the world. Our interactions gradually become characterized by greater tolerance, empathy, and love.

Ethnocentrism: The "We" Stage

As we progress from the self-focused, egocentric stage, our perspective begins to widen, ushering us into the realm of ethnocentrism. In this stage, the "me" transforms into "we," and our identity starts to align with the groups and communities we belong to.

Beginning around the age of seven, we typically start to develop a more profound understanding of the roles and emotions of others. This is when friendships become more significant, and experiences such as starting school introduce us to broader social dynamics. As we grow, our sense of identity gradually shifts from being centered solely on ourselves to being defined by our affiliation with a particular group.

The desire for acceptance and belonging becomes a driving force at this stage. The norms, beliefs, and traditions of the tribe—whether it's a family, a nation, a religious group, a political party, a sports team, a race, or an ethnic group—take on immense importance. Our sense of worth and identity becomes closely tied to how well we conform to and uphold the values of our group. Our tribe's beliefs and cultural practices become the lens through which we view the world.

A key characteristic of the ethnocentric stage of consciousness is the belief that our own group possesses a unique and often superior essence, setting it apart from others. This perspective divides the world into stark contrasts: us versus them, insiders versus outsiders, or allies versus adversaries. Such dichotomous thinking can foster feelings of superiority, disdain, or even hostility toward those who are not part of our group.

While the ethnocentric stage represents a step forward from the self-centeredness of the egocentric stage, it also harbors the potential for greater harm. When this collective identity hardens into a "collective ego," it can justify harmful or even violent actions as long as they are seen as protecting or advancing the tribe's interests. In extreme cases, this can lead to conflicts, wars, or acts of violence, all justified by the perceived need to defend the tribe's integrity or superiority.

Historically, religious beliefs and practices have often been shaped by this ethnocentric stage. The Old Testament, for example, portrays a God who, at times, supports the conquests and conflicts carried out by his chosen people, subtly reinforcing their sense of superiority. When Jesus introduced the idea of a universal, all-encompassing God who transcends tribal boundaries, his teachings directly challenged the prevailing ethnocentric views of his time, which ultimately led to his crucifixion.

We might hope that Christianity, inspired by Jesus's vision of universal love and unity, would move beyond ethnocentrism. However, history shows that this has not always been the case. The Crusades of the European Middle Ages, where Christians waged wars against Muslims in the name of God, are a stark example of how deeply entrenched ethnocentric views can be within religious contexts.

Regrettably, many people and societies around the world, including significant segments of Christianity, still remain deeply rooted in ethnocentric thinking. This is evident in persistent issues like sexism, racism, religious fundamentalism, and nationalism. In recent years, the rise of Christian Nationalism in the United States and extreme political movements exemplify how the stage of ethnocentric consciousness continues to shape modern society. These movements often blend religious fervor with nationalistic ideology, promoting the idea that their group —whether defined by religion, race, or political belief—is uniquely righteous or superior.

Christian Nationalism, for instance, interprets religious identity through the lens of national pride, often equating Christianity with specific political or cultural agendas. This viewpoint can lead to the exclusion or demonization of those who do not share the same beliefs or who belong to different ethnic, racial, or religious groups. Far-right and far-left movements, similarly, have capitalized on ethnocentric sentiments by fostering an "us versus them" mentality that pits one segment of society against another, often along the lines of race, immigration status, or political ideology.

Such movements highlight the dangers of ethnocentrism when it is taken to extremes. The belief that one's own worldview is the only true or valid perspective can result in a refusal to engage with others who hold different beliefs, creating deep divisions within society. These divisions can lead to social and political conflicts and, in some cases, to acts of violence that are justified as protecting the tribe or group from perceived threats.

World-centrism: The "Everybody" Stage

As we continue to evolve through the stages of consciousness, we begin to see that we are all connected. We start to recognize that our wellbeing is intrinsically linked to the wellbeing of others, extending far beyond our immediate surroundings. This marks our entry into the world-centric stage of consciousness, where our concern shifts from just our little corner of the world to the global community.

Often emerging during adolescence, this stage of consciousness prompts us to engage with reality from a broader, "everybody" viewpoint. The boundaries of ethnocentrism—where our identity was closely tied to specific groups—begin to dissolve, allowing us to develop a more universal understanding of the world. With this new perspective, we gain the ability to critically reflect on and challenge the cultural beliefs and traditions we once took for granted.

Though the world-centric lens is a relatively recent development in human history, it has become increasingly prevalent in modern society. Many people today, even if primarily ethnocentric in their orientation, are capable of adopting this more expansive viewpoint. Historically, this shift in consciousness has been the driving force behind significant societal revolutions, such as the abolition of slavery and the institutionalization of principles like human rights, equality, and freedom. It laid the foundation for a consensus against discrimination based on race, gender, creed, or sexuality.

This elevated consciousness also championed reason, giving birth to the modern scientific era. The comforts and innovations of contemporary life—from medical marvels to technological wonders—are direct products of this world-centric mindset. It is through this lens that humanity has made some of its greatest strides.

Yet, the world-centric stage is not a single, monolithic stage of consciousness. Within it, there are various sub-stages, each contributing to the broadening of our perspective. At its foundational level, often referred to as the **mythic-rational** stage, we begin to merge strong ethnocentric values with world-centric reasoning. This means that while we may still hold on to the deep-rooted beliefs and traditions of our group or culture, we start to apply rational thinking to these beliefs, questioning and adapting them to fit a more inclusive, global framework.[4]

In this stage, we are often still loyal to our cultural or religious traditions, but we are no longer bound by them in the same rigid way. We begin to recognize that while our own values are important, other worldviews also have validity. This leads to a greater openness and willingness to engage with different cultures, ideologies, and perspectives. Here, in the mythic-rational stage, we see the early signs of the shift from a "the beliefs of my group are the only truth" mindset to a more expansive understanding that acknowledges both the value of tradition and the importance of universality.

The next substage within the world-centric stage of consciousness is the **rational stage.** This stage is marked by a profound shift toward abstract thinking, systematic reasoning, and a deep reverence for the scientific method. In this phase, which typically emerges during our late teenage years, we begin to critically examine the world around us, no longer accepting things at face value. We start questioning the status quo, searching for concrete, evidence-based answers to life's mysteries. In this stage, truth is measured by empirical evidence, logical consistency, and coherent reasoning, making it a transformative step in human development.[5]

The influence of the rational mindset has profoundly shaped the modern world. It underpins the functioning of democratic governance, where laws and policies are debated and enacted based on reasoned argument and evidence. In the business world, multinational corporations thrive by employing strategic analysis, data-driven decisions, and methodical approaches rooted in rational thought. As we navigate this stage, we develop an insatiable curiosity to unravel the complexities of the world, using analytical tools not just to understand scientific phenomena but also to scrutinize cultural narratives and societal structures.

This rational exploration often leads to re-evaluating long-held beliefs inherited from family, culture, or religion. We begin to seek universally applicable truths, questioning traditions that may have once gone unchallenged. This stage fosters a more critical approach to life, where we aim to balance the wisdom of past teachings with the forward momentum of intellectual progress, always driven by the pursuit of knowledge and clarity.

Another sub-stage within the world-centric spectrum is the **pluralistic stage**, which emphasizes diversity, inclusivity, and global harmony. At this stage, we move beyond merely tolerating differences to fully recognizing that every culture, society, and individual contributes a unique and valuable perspective to the global community. It's not just about acknowledging the existence of diverse view-points; it's about actively embracing and celebrating them, understanding that these differences enhance the rich-ness of the human experience.[6]

Those who operate from a pluralistic perspective often prioritize critical global issues such as environmental sustainability, social equality, and human rights. They recognize that these challenges transcend national borders and require collective action. By valuing the diver-sity of worldviews, pluralistic individuals strive for a harmonious coexistence that honors the dignity and rights of all people, regardless of race, religion, gender, or nationality.

This mindset leads to open dialogue and collaboration across cultural and societal boundaries. Pluralistic indi-viduals are skilled at juggling multiple perspectives, constantly seeking a deeper understanding of how to bridge divides and create more inclusive communities. Their ability to view the world through multiple lenses enables them to navigate complex global challenges with a sense of empathy and a commitment to the greater good, striving to create a world where differences are not just accepted but celebrated as vital contributions to our shared humanity.

While the world-centric stage of consciousness is vast and inclusive, it is not without its internal tensions. Many of the cultural and political conflicts we see today are rooted in the friction between different sub-stages within world-centrism. For example, those who lean toward the rational sub-stage often place a high value on logic, empirical evidence, and personal achievements. From their perspective, pluralism can seem overly idealistic or impractical, especially when it challenges their emphasis on individual success and fiscal independence. They may argue that too much focus on inclusivity and diversity dilutes merit-based systems or slows economic progress.

On the other hand, those coming from a pluralistic perspective often see society as trapped in outdated structures driven by unchecked ambition, exclusion, and inequality. They emphasize the need for compassion, equity, and the dismantling of systems that have historically marginalized various groups. From their viewpoint, the rational focus on personal accomplishments and independence can seem cold and disconnected from the collective wellbeing. These opposing views often clash in debates about wealth distribution, climate change, immigration, and social justice, where rational thinkers may prioritize efficiency and economic growth, while pluralists push for greater social responsibility and environmental stewardship.

A poignant irony emerges within this world-centric stage. As we strive for inclusivity and a broader, more compassionate worldview, a new form of bias can quietly take root—this time, not based on traditional divisions like race, religion, or nationality, but on intellectual differences. For example, in our efforts to promote progressive values, we may become intolerant of those who hold more conservative or traditional beliefs. In the very act of championing openness and acceptance, there's a risk of alienating or dismissing those whose worldviews don't align with our own, labeling them as ignorant or backward.

We see this irony play out in contemporary culture wars, especially online, where debates about topics like climate change, social justice, or healthcare quickly become polarized. While the pluralistic camp may call for inclusivity, they might unintentionally exclude voices from the rational or more conservative perspectives, accusing them of being out of touch or insensitive. In doing so, the goal of inclusivity itself can be undermined by creating new divisions based on intellectual or ideological grounds.

Despite its internal tensions, the world-centric stage has produced numerous positive outcomes. One of the most visible signs of its impact is the rise of countless charitable organizations dedicated to addressing global challenges like poverty, hunger, and climate change. These organizations, from large-scale efforts like the Red Cross to smaller grassroots initiatives, represent a collective drive toward bettering the world for all people, regardless of race, nationality, or religion. Individuals, many of whom have experienced spiritual awakenings or moments of deep personal reflection, often feel called to leverage their talents, time, and resources to uplift humanity as a whole. This mindset transcends traditional boundaries, reflecting a commitment to serving the global community rather than just one's own.

A powerful example of this shift can be seen within Christianity, particularly through the progressive church movement. This movement embodies the pluralistic phase of world-centrism by actively embracing inclusivity and diversity. Progressive churches welcome people from all walks of life, offering a space where traditional religious beliefs are expanded to include a deeper exploration of life's mysteries. These churches often prioritize social justice, environmental stewardship, and the affirmation of LGBTQ+ communities, creating a sanctuary for spiritual seekers who may have felt marginalized by more traditional faith environments.

By championing inclusivity, the progressive church challenges its members to rethink the boundaries of faith, inviting everyone to engage in a journey of spiritual growth that transcends creed, race, or background. This reflects the broader world-centric shift toward unity and collective wellbeing, where the focus moves from "us versus them" to a deeper understanding of our shared human experience. The fruits of this stage are seen not only in these spiritual communities but also in the broader world as more people come together to address global challenges with compassion, collaboration, and a commitment to inclusivity.

The "One" Stage: Beyond Dualities to Unity

The initial stages of consciousness—the egocentric, ethnocentric, and world-centric inner maps—are well understood today. Each stage expands our awareness from a focus on ourselves to a broader connection with others and the world. However, a deeper "One" stage, sometimes called *"Christ-consciousness,"* remains less familiar. This stage transcends intellectual understanding and represents a continuous awareness of our oneness with God and creation. Unlike momentary experiences of connection, Christ-consciousness is a lived reality where we fully embrace our true self beyond the ego.

Throughout this book, we've explored the awakening to a deeper dimension within us, beyond the ego-self. This awakening nurtures a profound sense of unity with all life and a connection to higher wisdom. As the mind begins to transform—much like Paul's description of having the "mind of Christ"—it becomes less driven by ego and more attuned to the wisdom that flows through the heart. Our actions are increasingly grounded in humility, gratitude, and grace.

At a certain point, we may move beyond ego-driven stages and enter the One stage of consciousness. This stage reflects the lasting integration of a state of consciousness we may have experienced temporarily before—where dualities like "me" versus "you" or "us" versus "them" are transcended. In this stage, the awareness of oneness with all existence becomes a natural and enduring part of our everyday experience. Each being and moment is recognized as a reflection of the divine, transforming our life and bringing with it a deep and sustained sense of peace, joy, and purpose. Free from the ego's constraints, we embody the oneness that has always been waiting to be fully realized.

It's helpful to revisit our understanding of God to more fully grasp this concept of Christ-consciousness. Of course, the mystery of God is beyond our human comprehension. Any attempt to define God, or even Christ, within the confines of a book will always fall short. The best we can do is draw from our limited knowledge, traditional spiritual wisdom, and personal experiences to form an understanding. Even then, this understanding is only a glimpse of the infinite, a way to point toward something that remains ultimately unknowable in its fullness.

Yet, even as we acknowledge the mystery of God, it is human nature to seek understanding, to try to express the inexpressible. By attempting to describe God, we are not necessarily confining the divine to our definitions but engaging in a process of exploration, using language and symbols as tools to help us connect with the divine mystery. These explanations are not meant to contain God but to open our hearts and minds to deeper truths.

In this book, I've referred to God as the *"One-Life"*—the boundless, unifying consciousness that underlies all of existence. Through quantum physics, we learn that particles—the very core of physical matter—emerge from a wave state when observed. This suggests that observation, and therefore consciousness, plays a fundamental role in bringing reality into form. How could something be observed without consciousness behind it? In this way, I propose that God is the ultimate, limitless consciousness where all dualities dissolve. God is both immanent (present within all things) and transcendent (existing beyond all things). At the deepest level, God is the unified field of consciousness that pervades and connects everything in the universe.

Another way to express this understanding of God is through the concept of *Being* or the *Ground of Being*. Here, consciousness is seen as the foundation of all that exists. God, then, is not a separate entity or being, but the very essence of awareness from which everything arises. This divine consciousness is what sustains life and allows us to experience the world around us. It is the Ground of Being that supports all existence.

Some refer to God as *Source,* emphasizing the divine as the infinite presence and energy that flows through all creation. In this view, everything—including our awareness—emerges from this divine Source. Mystics remind us that the Source is not distant or abstract, but intimately connected to our daily experience of life. We are expressions of this divine consciousness, inseparable from the Source that gives life to all things.

This view is different from pantheism, which claims that everything *is* God. Instead, this perspective suggests that everything is *connected to* God, with God being the presence that underlies and supports all existence. As Paul beautifully stated, "In God, we live, move, and have our being," reminding us of our inseparable connection to the divine presence in every aspect of life.

What Is Christ-Consciousness?

Many of us might recall the religious teachings in which Christ is understood as the embodiment of divine essence in human form. God transcends creation while yet incarnating in it as Christ. Jesus is, therefore, described as Christ because his followers saw in him the essence of God manifesting through his form.

Yet, there is another biblical and mystical perspective, one that expands the scope of Christ beyond just the historical figure of Jesus. According to this view, Christ is present throughout all creation. From the moment of the universe's inception—what science calls the Big Bang—Christ has been manifest within all things. The eternal One-Life, transcendent and formless, became incarnate within the universe as Christ. This understanding of Christ as the divine force in all creation invites us to see the sacred in everything around us, from the stars in the sky to the smallest flower, all infused with divine essence.

This broader view of Christ is eloquently captured by Pierre Teilhard de Chardin, a Jesuit priest, mystic, and paleontologist. Teilhard proposed that Christ is not only the *Alpha*—the beginning—but also the *Omega,* the final point toward which all creation is evolving. In Teilhard's vision, Christ is the divine agent orchestrating the evolutionary unfolding of

creation. He spoke of Christ "putting himself in the position...to purify, to direct, to super-animate the general
ascent of consciousness into which he inserted himself."[7]

This means Christ, through divine love and wisdom, is
constantly moving creation toward greater awareness of
its divine essence, guiding us all toward that final Omega
Point where we are conscious that everything is united
in God.

In Christian mysticism, this ascent of consciousness finds
its highest expression in the person of Jesus, who was
fully conscious of his divine essence. Through his life and
teachings, Jesus embodied the selfless love that transcends the ego and heals all division, making him an
archetype for all creation. His message was not just about
individual salvation but about the transformation of all
humanity, a call to awaken to our unity with God and each
other.

This love was perhaps most evident in Jesus's final
moments on the cross, when, in the face of immense
suffering, he prayed for forgiveness for his persecutors.
His words, "Forgive them, for they know not what they
do,"[8] reveal a profound understanding of the unity of all
things. Jesus recognized that the people who crucified
him were acting out of ignorance, their awareness
clouded by ego and fear. They were unable to see the
divine presence within themselves and within him. Yet,
even in the midst of this, Jesus responded with compas-

sion, demonstrating the depth of his Christ-consciousness.

Throughout his life, Jesus consistently aligned himself with those marginalized, rejected, and wounded by society. He reached out to the poor, the sick, and the outcast, not from a place of pity but from a profound recognition of their shared humanity. Jesus knew that his identity was not separate from theirs; he saw himself in them and them in him. This deep sense of interconnectedness is the essence of Christ-consciousness, the realization that we are all part of the same divine whole.

From this, it becomes apparent that Christ-consciousness is the evolution of our soul, a profound inner awareness of Christ as the unifying essence of God within us and all else. As we ascend into this stage of consciousness, we begin to perceive the presence of Christ not as an external force but as the unifying essence that flows through all things. This awakening fosters a profound sense of connection and unity with God, moving us beyond the confines of egoic separation into a deeper understanding of our interconnectedness with all life.

Mystics often describe this stage as one of profound awakening. It is a shift where the boundaries between "self" and "other" blur, and the sense of separation begins to fade until it dissolves completely. We no longer see ourselves as isolated individuals. Instead, we experience life as a seamless, interconnected whole. The mystical experience of nonduality is characterized by an intimate awareness that everything we encounter is infused with the same divine presence—nothing is separate from God, and therefore, nothing is separate from us.

One of the most powerful metaphors for this nondual consciousness is that of the ocean and the wave. The ocean symbolizes the eternal, unchanging essence of existence—God—while the wave represents our individual selves, constantly in flux, rising and falling, appearing to be separate but always a part of the greater whole. In Christ-consciousness, we understand that while the wave may seem distinct from the ocean, it is never truly separate. The wave is an expression of the ocean, just as we are an expression of God. In this state of awareness, we recognize that our true nature is not confined to the individual wave but is deeply connected to the infinite ocean of divine presence.

This awareness transcends mere intellectual understanding; it is a deeper knowing, rooted in stillness. In contrast to the earlier stages of egocentric, ethnocentric, and world-centric consciousness—each of which is tied to the conditioned mind and shaped by fear, desire, and division —Christ-consciousness is anchored in the timeless, formless essence of God that animates our being. It is a return to our true nature beyond the limitations of the mind and ego.

As we transition from fear-based stages of consciousness into Christ-consciousness, we do not reject or judge the stages we have passed through. Instead, we carry the wisdom and empathy gained from each stage. Our journey through these various stages of consciousness has shaped us, and we now integrate that knowledge into a life centered on love, humility, and forgiveness. We no longer see others as separate or different, but as part of the same divine fabric. Our actions are motivated by care, compassion, and grace, as we recognize the presence of God in everything and everyone we encounter.

In this stage, our life becomes a luminous beacon, radiating the light of Christ-consciousness. We embody the qualities of wisdom, creativity, and grace, navigating the complexities of life with a deep awareness of our unity with all of creation. As Jesus said, "You are the light of the world." Through Christ-consciousness, we shine this light, illuminating the path for others to follow, reflecting the divine essence in every thought, word, and action.

In the rest of the book, we will explore practical ways to actively become conscious of the divine presence—Christ in us—in our daily lives so that this transformation can unfold fully. By doing so, we can contribute to the greater good and experience profound spiritual and mental well-being, living in harmony with the divine presence within and around us.

9

THE HEART AS A CONDUIT

Meditation has recently become a widely accepted practice in the Western world, yet its roots run deep in Eastern traditions, where it has been embraced for centuries, even millennia. Beyond its Eastern origins, meditation has also played a vital role in the mystical traditions of Christianity, Judaism, and Islam. The essential purpose of meditation is to cultivate inner stillness, a heightened awareness that brings us into a state of peace and presence.

A similar practice found within Christian mysticism is known as contemplation. Unlike more structured forms of prayer or intellectual reflection, contemplation invites the soul to rest directly in God's presence, transcending thoughts, concepts, and images. It is often described as a way of experiencing God in the silence of the heart—beyond words and rituals—entering into a state of pure, loving communion with Christ. This silent union is sometimes referred to as "the prayer of the heart" or "silent love."

For the sake of simplicity, throughout this book, I've referred to both meditation and contemplation as "meditation," since the essence of both practices is strikingly similar. Before I dive into the core principles of our meditation practice, let me share a bit about my own journey with meditation and how it led to the development of the techniques I now share with others.

I was first introduced to meditation in early 2006, as detailed in Chapter 3. The idea of meditation was initially entirely alien, even intimidating. But one day, as I walked down a set of stairs, overwhelmed by relentless cluster headaches, I felt a sudden, almost mystical pull to meditate. With no prior knowledge, experience, or even an inkling toward meditation, I settled into the seat of my black Nissan Maxima, closed my eyes, and focused on a scene from the story of Jesus that depicted unconditional love. In that moment, a wave of profound love washed over me, and the pain dissipated. The despair and heaviness that had consumed me vanished in an instant.

Since that transformative experience, my understanding of meditation has deepened substantially. I've realized its ultimate purpose is to enter a state of inner stillness, where we are fully present and free from the mental noise of thoughts and negative emotions.

As I began to embrace meditation regularly, I found myself less burdened by anxiety, worry, and stress. My blood pressure markedly improved, and my overall well-being elevated to levels I hadn't felt in ages. Moreover, lingering feelings of guilt and fear began to fade, and most of my prior insecurities waned. Returning to that state of inner stillness has that profound impact on our minds and bodies.

In 2012, I developed a forty-day meditation initiative. Before its official release, a Dutch friend expressed interest in a sneak peek. Initially hesitant, due to concerns about how it would be received, I nevertheless eventually sent him the audio files. Three short weeks later, he called me to enthusiastically detail its transformative effect on his life. In a remarkably short span, he introduced hundreds to the program across multiple continents. Since then, our meditation programs have been translated into Dutch, Spanish, and Swahili. Today, it's embraced across Africa, Europe, Asia, South America, and North America, guiding individuals toward a deep connection with divine love.

The testimonials from individuals transformed by these meditation exercises have surpassed my wildest expectations. Whether it was Lois, a woman raised as an orphan who used the meditations to help her overcome decades of nightly nightmares, or Richard, who used them to cure many years of insomnia, these simple daily exercises have worked for many because these meditations were

designed to amplify awareness of inner peace and unconditional love.

A particularly remarkable account is from a young
mother named Debbie, who had been diagnosed with
terminal brain cancer. Initially skeptical, Debbie started
practicing the meditations and soon became deeply
moved by an intense and pure sense of love. Six months
later, a routine brain scan revealed that her tumor had
vanished, and all cancer symptoms had receded. Her
doctor subsequently confirmed her complete return to
health.

Over time, my personal meditation has grown profoundly
deeper in both peace and love. This journey led us to
create HeartFaith, a daily meditation routine. Wherever
this unique practice has taken root, we've witnessed
remarkable transformations. I hope it will do the same for
you. In this chapter, I will explain the core principles
behind HeartFaith meditations, and in the next chapter,
I'll guide you through a simple, step-by-step meditative
practice that anyone can follow.

HeartFaith Meditation

HeartFaith meditation draws inspiration from the wisdom
of Jesus, aiming to create a deep sense of harmony within us.
At its core, it's about entering a state of heart coherence—
where our heart, mind, and soul are perfectly aligned and in
tune with the infinite consciousness or spirit. However, this

meditation isn't just a practice. It's a pathway to expanding our view of life, enhancing our connections with the world, and deepening our understanding of ourselves and others.

When we reach this state of harmony, our brains operate at their best. This isn't just about feeling good. It's about boosting our mental functions to their maximum potential. You'll find yourself processing information more efficiently, making decisions with greater clarity, and tackling complex problems with newfound ease. It sharpens your focus, turning challenges that once seemed overwhelming into manageable tasks, and elevates your ability to think critically and creatively.

But the benefits of heart coherence go beyond just cognitive improvements. It fundamentally changes how we experience and manage our emotions. Instead of being swept away by strong feelings or reacting on impulse, this balanced state allows for a clearer, more stable view of our emotional landscape. This helps us navigate our personal lives with more grace and enhances our relationships. By fostering more transparent communication and a deeper understanding, heart coherence strengthens our connections with others, making for more meaningful interactions and bonds.

This state of balance profoundly impacts our physical wellbeing too. When our bodies operate from a place of coherence, they're better equipped to fend off illnesses, thanks to an enhanced immune response. This heightened defense system not only makes us more resilient against diseases but also aids in a faster recovery when health setbacks occur.

Now, let's bridge the gap between this concept and faith. Typically, the word "faith" brings to mind adherence to religious beliefs, moral codes, or specific rituals. This conventional perspective on faith might seem at odds with the idea of heart coherence. However, the key to connecting these dots lies in understanding the difference between traditional faith—often rooted in intellectual acceptance or cultural practice—and heart faith, which is deeply experiential and transformative.

HeartFaith Is Not an Alignment with Religious Doctrines

HeartFaith transcends mere intellectual agreement with religious doctrines or moral principles. It invites us into a deeper, more intrinsic form of faith that the mind cannot fully capture.

The human brain, a marvel of evolution, is divided into three primary areas: the cerebral cortex, the limbic system, and the cerebellum. The cerebral cortex, the brain's outermost layer, is the powerhouse of conscious thought, responsible for our higher cognitive functions, like reasoning, language, memory, and creativity. This part of the brain plays a pivotal role in shaping our knowledge and understanding of the world.

It's tempting to locate faith within the cerebral cortex, attributing it to intellectual assent or alignment with a specific set of beliefs. This perspective sees faith as an exercise in mental agreement, a conscious choice to accept a particular narrative or doctrine as truth. However, this intellectualized view of faith limits it to a rigid framework, confining our spirituality to predefined mental concepts and narratives. While some narratives may hold greater accuracy than others, this form of faith often falls short of transforming lives in a meaningful way. Rather than fostering profound change, it tends to entrench us in ethnocentrism and a religion rooted in fear, limiting the expansive potential of our spirituality.

In contrast, the wisdom of Jesus and the teaching of certain other traditions within the Semitic lineage offer a different vision of faith. They present faith not as an intellectual exercise but as a heartfelt knowing, a profound intuition that transcends rational thought. This form of faith is experiential, rooted in a deep connection with God and an inherent understanding of universal love beyond words or doctrines. It's about living in a state of peace and compassion, embracing a connectedness with all of life rather than adhering strictly to specific dogmas.

HeartFaith Is Not Rooted in Emotions

While many associate the heart with emotions, it's essential to differentiate between the two. Indeed, our emotions influence our heart, leading to heart-rate variability and transmitting stress signals throughout our body. However, emotions primarily arise from the limbic system beneath the cerebral cortex. Often referred to as the "emotional brain," the limbic system encompasses various structures pivotal to emotion, motivation, and memory. It plays a crucial role in our emotional interpretation of the environment, storing and retrieving emotional memories and regulating our interactions with the world.

A vital component of the limbic system is the amygdala, which is pivotal in processing emotions, particularly those linked to fear. Upon sensing danger, the amygdala can initiate the body's fight-or-flight response, priming an individual for swift reactions. The amygdala gathers sensory data from the thalamus, interprets this information, and liaises with different brain regions, including the prefrontal cortex, hippocampus, and brainstem, to guide behavior, physical reactions, and emotional states.[1]

When we connect faith with emotions, it's often tied to underlying fears. For instance, the fear of death or the afterlife might lead someone toward a religious path, as they hope to mitigate those anxieties. Emotions like guilt and shame can also propel an individual toward specific religious beliefs. While this is commonly referred to as "finding faith," it's crucial to understand that this type of faith is anchored in the brain's limbic system, not genuinely emanating from the heart.

Faith and the Ego

From a more philosophical or spiritual perspective, emotions emanate from the egoic mind. As noted earlier, this state perpetually aims to differentiate itself, often by measuring our worth against others. Anchored in a pervasive sense of inadequacy or the feeling of not being "enough," faith can adopt a self-serving hue under the influence of this egoic mind. When interwoven with the analytical functions of the prefrontal cortex, faith can inadvertently become a yardstick, a tool for comparison, positioning ourselves in relation to others.

When a desired outcome unfolds after prayer, it's easy to attribute it to our faith. "I prayed in faith, and God answered me" becomes the narrative. The ego subtly but swiftly intervenes, painting us as favored: "God heard *my* prayer because of *my* faith." This narrative subtly elevates us, setting us apart from others whose prayers might not have been answered. Underlying this is a quiet emotional surge that makes "me" feel special.

Yet, when prayers are seemingly not answered, the ego demands an explanation that alleviates feelings of not being enough for God to answer our prayers. The blame frequently lands on external factors. It might be chalked up to God's grand plan, an assault from darker forces, the current spiritual climate, societal sins, or even the perceived spiritual deficits of those close to us.

Alternatively, there are moments when individuals internalize the perceived failure, pinning unanswered prayers on their own lack of faith, personal sins, or some other perceived misstep. Though it appears self-critical, this introspection indirectly bolsters the ego, casting the individual as a silent martyr or victim.

These various presumptions about faith stem from a perception of duality, wherein God is perceived as a distinct entity, separate from us. This perspective imagines an external God bestowing blessings upon some and withholding from others. Under this belief, it's surmised that our desires—be it for salvation, prosperity, freedom, etc.—are granted based on our righteousness and prayers, the authenticity of our belief, or our affiliation with a particular religious institution or group.

Such a viewpoint paints God as capricious and limited, leading skeptics to see this deity as a projection of the human ego crafted to endorse one person or group's superiority over others. This God, shaped in our image, validates those who are similar to us while condemning those who are different. Given our broad knowledge about the vastness and nature of the universe, this constrained belief becomes increasingly untenable for many, often driving a wedge between them and organized religion.

On the other hand, the faith of the heart transcends mere intellect and logic. When faith is distilled to a belief system or creed, it is susceptible to the ego's manipulation, ensnaring us in the mirage of separateness. While faith can indeed be discussed and articulated, its essence evades mere intellectual comprehension. Jesus emphasized that faith is innate in the heart. It offers a vision beyond the ego's narrow scope. This kind of faith of the heart is an awareness of a transcendent Presence manifesting as boundless love. Through this enlightened lens, we become aware of our true nature and our unity with God.

The notion of invoking God to steer our lives isn't then about the ego's whimsical attempts to elicit responses based on faith or prayers. Instead, better health, profound joy, creativity, inner wellbeing, and increased intelligence are the organic consequences of embracing awareness of our unity and oneness with God and one another.

Faith of the Heart

Throughout history, spiritual and religious traditions around the world have spoken about this kind of faith that emanates from the heart. This transcendent form of belief is not intellectual or fear-based but rather an innate, profound awareness or connection with God or a transcendent Presence.

For example, many indigenous cultures worldwide see the heart as a bridge between the earthly and spiritual realms —a place of intuition, wisdom, and connection to nature. One of the central prayers in Judaism starts with, "Hear, O Israel: The Lord our God, the Lord is One. And you shall love the Lord your God with all your heart, with all your soul, and with all your might."[2] This highlights the importance of heart-centered faith and devotion in Jewish tradition. For Buddhists, genuine faith stems from a heart free of attachments, aversions, and ignorance. Sufis believe the heart can be a direct receptor of divine grace.

The New Testament often equates the heart with a person's innermost being, the place from which faith, trust, and love spring forth. The Bible frequently speaks of "believing with the heart."

Jesus emphasized a faith that's rooted in the heart and untainted by doubt. In its original context, "doubt" wasn't about intellectual skepticism. Instead, a lack of doubt described an inner freedom from accusatory voices that judge, criticize, and condemn us as not being enough the way we are. This means that a heart liberated from doubt resonates with a sense of harmony and coherence, aligning with the vibrational dimension of the kingdom of God.

In this harmonious state, the heart transforms into a conduit of love and peace. This echoes what we discussed earlier: The divine breath, *ruach*, and the radiant light of God encounter no resistance in a heart that is in harmony. As a result, our inner essence, or *nephsha*, becomes vividly aware of Christ's omnipresent nature, discerning the divine essence in every aspect of creation.

This alignment lets the empowering "I can" of God echo within us, making the seemingly unattainable achievable. Echoing Jesus's words, with such faith, we can command the mountain to move, and it shall. However, Jesus's metaphor of moving mountains was not a call to flaunt divine powers. Instead, he was illuminating a state of being where we channel the intrinsic wisdom, vision, and energy of God and the universe, driven not by ego but by a profound love for all existence.

In this ascending state, our actions transform from merely human endeavors to divine expressions. Like a leaf that dances with the wind, not against it, we too learn to move in harmony with the greater rhythm of life. This isn't about bending reality to our will but aligning our will with what the Source of Life ordains. When we do so, miracles aren't just possible—they become the natural outcome of living in proper alignment with the spiritual tide that connects all beings.

Such alignment is akin to a musician being perfectly in tune with the orchestra. It's no longer about standing out as a solitary figure but becoming part of a grand symphony. Here, our most minor acts take on profound significance: a kind smile, a helping hand, a moment of understanding. These are not just acts of human kindness. They are what the Bible refers to as Christ-in-you expressing boundless love through us. In this way, we do not move mountains by force but by transforming each pebble of kindness into a pathway over which the impossible becomes possible.

Faith of the Heart Through Meditation

One essential question often arises when discussing HeartFaith: How do we cultivate such faith? At the core of this cultivation is the practice of meditation. As David, the shepherd who became King of Israel, beautifully expressed, meditation is the pathway to connect with the heart. In Psalm 4, he wrote, "Meditate within your heart... and be still."

Think of meditation like tuning a radio. When the dial is turned just right, the music flows clearly, free of static. In the same way, meditation helps you tune out the noise of the egoic mind, creating a quiet space between thoughts. In that space, awareness stands alone—pure, untouched. This is the "I am" that lives beyond names, beyond forms —your true self. In this moment of pure awareness, stillness rises from within. It has no shape, no form. It is spirit. It is the true "I am."

In that still, thoughtless moment, when you are aware of awareness itself, you experience yourself as something deeper: pure presence, loving and peaceful. Picture this deep "I am" like a wave on the surface of the ocean— unique, distinct, and fleeting. Yet, when you look closer, you see the wave is never separate from the ocean. It belongs to the vast, unified whole. And just like the wave, your true self is never separate from God but an emanation of the divine. Through stillness, through meditation, we awaken to this truth—that just as the wave is part of the ocean, we are inseparable from God's essence.

So, when the psalmist says, "Be still, and know that I am God," it is a gentle call to remember: In stillness, we touch our oneness with God. Just as the wave recognizes it is one with the ocean, we come to know that our true self emerges from and always remains a part of the One-Life.

Although traditional Christianity has not placed much emphasis on meditation, there is ample evidence that it was practiced in the early church. Over the centuries, Christian mystics have also spoken of similar practices like contemplation or centering prayer. Friar John Main, for example, advocated for centering prayer, focusing on a word or phrase to invite God's presence into the heart. Mystics like St. Ignatius, Guigo II, Teresa of Ávila, and Thomas Merton emphasized contemplative practices rooted in God's love, which fostered a sense of unity with the divine.

Throughout this book, I've touched on the transformative power of meditation. I hope it's clear how essential meditation is for attuning ourselves to the transcendent presence that permeates reality. It leads us into a harmonious alignment of heart, mind, soul, and body, as Jesus taught.

Now, let's move on to a practical method of HeartFaith meditation that's simple and accessible.

10

THE MELODY WITHIN

A famous luthier crafted exquisite violins in a distant town renowned for its musical prowess. One day, a distraught musician approached him, saying, "Despite playing this violin for years, it sounds out of tune, and I can't find harmony." The luthier gently took the violin, felt its core, and slightly adjusted the bridge and strings. Handing it back, he said, "Sometimes, the instrument is perfect, but it needs to be realigned with its core to produce the most harmonious melodies."

Similarly, I hope you'll experience the meditation practice introduced in this chapter as your personal luthier—helping you tune into the profound, harmonious rhythms of your deepest essence. Just as the luthier's touch restored the violin's melody, this practice gently realigns your heart, mind, and soul with the core of who you truly are. It assists you in moving beyond the tumultuous sea of emotions and thoughts, bringing your awareness into harmony with the deep peace and love intrinsic to your true self.

Imagine for a moment your thoughts and emotions like the strings of a violin. When the strings are too tight or too loose, they produce dissonance and a sense of disharmony. In much the same way, when our minds are cluttered with anxious thoughts or weighed down by emotional burdens, we lose the ability to perceive the deeper harmony that exists within us. HeartFaith meditation is like the gentle hand of the luthier, helping us realign the strings of our mind, heart, and soul so that the music of inner stillness, love, and wholeness can flow through us effortlessly.

This meditation goes beyond simply calming the surface-level turbulence of thoughts. It helps to create harmony between the brain's conscious and subconscious realms. Through this process, a subtle yet profound transformation occurs: an outdated way of viewing, being, and engaging with the world evolves into a more expansive, holistic approach to understanding reality and living life. This practice opens the doorway to a deeper sense of clarity, purpose, and connection—not only within ourselves but with the world around us.

As you continue with this practice, you may start to notice subtle yet profound changes in how you experience life. The constant chatter of the mind begins to quiet down, emotions feel lighter, and a new sense of alignment starts to emerge. You'll find yourself more present, more aware of the stillness that exists beneath everything, and more deeply connected to the love at the core of who you are. Like a finely tuned violin, your inner life will start to resonate with a deeper, more beautiful melody—a melody that has always been within you, just waiting to be heard.

Gratitude

When preparing for meditation, selecting a peaceful and private space is helpful. My preference is to meditate in my backyard, embraced by the splendor and serenity of nature. However, the key is to find a quiet, undisturbed space that suits your preferences.

As for posture, find a comfortable seated position that supports your body and allows you to relax. I favor the lotus position for its benefits to the back and shoulders. While some may prefer complete silence or the ambient sounds of nature, others might find soft meditation music or guided sessions more conducive. (On my website, davidyoungren.com, you'll find a free meditation without background music, while many of the meditations in our other programs include soothing background music to enhance the experience.)

Begin your meditation by grounding yourself in gratitude. Reflect on the various elements of your life, from the seemingly mundane, like the air you breathe, to the more profound, such as the love of family and friends. This gratitude practice paves the way for deeper connection and openness in your meditation.

Gratitude transcends mere words or thoughts. It's an internal feeling of fullness, an expansion within, and a heartfelt opening. It helps shift your focus from blaming or labeling things as good or evil to a wholehearted appreciation of life. This approach doesn't invalidate your experiences but instead frees you from seeing them through a lens of fear. By embracing gratitude, you move beyond judgment and awaken to the presence within.

Remember that you are more than the sum of your past experiences. The ego may hold onto these as defining, but you reduce their emotional hold over you by entering a state of gratitude.

This practice becomes more effortless with regular meditation. After a minute or more in a state of gratitude, close your eyes and breathe deeply. Inhale for around four seconds, hold the breath for another two to three seconds, then exhale slowly for five to six seconds. Repeat this pattern for at least one minute, though aiming for five minutes is ideal for deeper benefits.

These deep breaths aid in centering yourself in the present moment and enhancing calmness. Keep your focus on your breathing, continually rooted in gratitude.

Be aware that distractions may occur. There might be times when the temptation to stop meditating becomes strong, and you might occasionally succumb to it. This is a natural part of the process. With consistent practice, meditation will become more instinctive and fluid.

Attentive to Peace in Meditation

As you transition into paying attention to peace during meditation, let the warmth of gratitude envelop you, soothing your mind and softening your thoughts. This next phase is about tuning in to awareness of inner still-ness, visualizing it as a serene wave that gently calms and brings balance to your entire being.

Chronic stress can significantly deplete your energy and lead to physical symptoms like headaches, muscle tension, chest pain, fatigue, sleep disturbances, stomach issues, and changes in libido. These symptoms often hinder a deep awareness of the presence within. It's essential to release physical tightness and nervous tension, guiding your body back to peace, rest, and harmony.

Begin by focusing on your breath, and then envision peace flowing through your digestive system, coursing down your body, back up again through your brain, and finally settling in your heart. Pay attention to each body part and feel any tension that exists. When you detect tension, breathe out, release it, and allow peace to settle.

Consider integrating Jesus's words into the meditation if you are a Christian. Simply visualize Jesus before you, imparting his calming words: "Peace, I leave you. My peace I give unto you... Let not your heart be troubled, neither let it be afraid."[1] You may also recall Jesus's post-resurrection words to his followers: "Peace be with you.... Receive the Holy Spirit."[2]

This imagery serves as a guidepost and reminder that your body, which biblical accounts describe as the temple of the Holy Spirit, is a vessel for unconditioned and pure consciousness. Then, softly move deeper than thought into a state of awareness of peace flowing through you, easing tension and stress.

Keep in mind that words act as guides, leading you toward an awareness of the inner loving presence. Dwelling too much on mental concepts and stories can make your mind overly busy, allowing thoughts to take over your consciousness. This can unintentionally revive the ego during meditation, nurturing a false sense of spiritual elitism and the belief that you are more enlightened or uniquely chosen when compared to others.

Make this meditative practice part of your daily routine. Initially, it might be challenging, but continually entering a state of inner stillness is vital. Regularly cultivating peace in your body can reduce stress levels, improve immune function, and improve overall health.

Unconditional Love

Deepening your meditation by integrating a focus on unconditional love can pave the way for healing the shadows within your subconscious and mending relationships. Our subconscious is filled with patterns driven by ego and its fears, which create a sense of separation between ourselves and the world around us. The story of Adam and Eve and the Tree of Knowledge of Good and Evil symbolizes this division, embedding deep notions of "good versus evil," "right versus wrong," and, ultimately, an "us versus them" mentality. We often see our perspectives as correct, observing differing views or people through a lens of judgment.

Judgmental patterns don't just create walls between us and others—they also cause us to disconnect from parts of ourselves. We tend to push away uncomfortable feelings, drawing lines we're afraid to cross because we don't want to face our pain. This avoidance often traps harrowing memories stained with shame—the kind of shame that tells us we're not just flawed in what we do but somehow unworthy at our core. Shame doesn't just linger; it seeps into our identity, casting shadows that shape how we see ourselves and influence our actions, often leading to deep mental and emotional struggles.

But there's a way out. By bringing unconditional love into your meditation practice, you can begin to break free from these patterns. Embracing love in your daily meditation is a powerful, healing journey. It helps lift the weight of past burdens and opens the door to a more compassionate connection with yourself and others, transforming how you see and experience life.

Jesus is often regarded as the embodiment of unconditional love for Christians, deeply aware of his oneness
with God and unbound by ego. His declaration, "The
Father and I are one," reflects his profound awareness of a
reality beyond the physical realm, recognizing his true self
—the profound "I am"—beyond earthly limitations. For
Jesus, being one with God and seeing himself in "the least
of these" was not just a theological concept but a way of
viewing reality through the eyes of God. This awareness of
love beyond mental constructs transformed his thoughts,
emotions, and habits. Love infused every part of his being,
not only his heart but also his brain, including the limbic
system and cerebellum.

In the face of crucifixion, Jesus displayed a peace that
transcended human understanding. He was not weighed
down by his challenging past or troubled by material
concerns. When betrayed and rejected by close companions like Peter, he did not respond with offense,
vengeance, or bitterness. Instead, he facilitated healing.
His continual expression of unconditional love was not
driven by obligation or religious duty but flowed naturally
from his innermost being.

From Jesus, we learn that unconditional love is the ultimate counter to the ego. It opens our hearts to the divine
ruach (spirit), fostering deeper heart coherence. When
love saturates our subconscious, it acts as a healing balm
for past traumas and painful memories, rewriting our
inner narrative. It shifts our self-identity from one dominated by the ego to one aligned with the transcending

presence. In Jesus, we see the transformative power of love —not only to heal and unify but to redefine our very existence beyond the limitations of the ego.

Integrating unconditional love into meditation is a pathway to experiencing this "spirit of love," not as a theological concept but as an inner awareness that heals and transforms our instincts, attitudes, and habits. This process fosters inner peace, reducing resistance to the present moment and enabling us to perceive each moment with gratitude.

To effectively integrate love into your meditation, start by cultivating an atmosphere of unconditional love. While love goes beyond what words can express, language and imagery can help set the stage for a deeply loving experience.

I experienced this firsthand during the time when I was struggling with intense cluster headaches. I realized that these physical symptoms were deeply connected to personal shame I had tried to suppress. I had compartmentalized painful parts of my past, pushing them aside, but the emotional barriers I had built were showing up in my body. During meditation, I revisited a scene from the movie *The Passion of the Christ* that, to me, embodied the essence of unconditional love. Immersed in that atmosphere, I had a transformative moment where I felt profoundly loved without conditions—it was as if the shame I had carried melted away, and, remarkably, the intense pain immediately subsided.

This experience taught me that stories and concepts illustrating love can help us cultivate that same atmosphere in our meditation. But it's important to remember that this awareness of love goes beyond the stories or words that guide us to it. It's not just a mental concept or story—it's a living, loving presence that rises from within, touching every part of our being and bringing healing from the inside out.

As you meditate, allow this loving presence to gently touch your past traumas and inner shadows. Acknowledge the pain rooted in your subconscious and let the sense of love soften its impact. This approach dissolves the internal barriers that cause inner conflict, creating harmony between your heart, mind, and soul.

This isn't about reliving past traumas but recognizing the roots of any inner resistance or discomfort and letting unconditional love transform those memories, removing the shame surrounding them.

For those with a Christian background, imagine Jesus as the embodiment of unconditional love. Picture his boundless love flowing into your heart, breaking down barriers and easing any resistance you feel. Whether this transformation happens instantly or unfolds over time, keep returning to this space of love, where your mental and emotional walls can come down, leading to profound changes in your instincts and behaviors.

This practice of embracing love also transforms your relationships. When faced with judgment, feelings of superiority or inferiority, or difficulty forgiving, bring unconditional love into your meditation. Let it shine on those emotions and relationships, guiding the healing process. This will ease your inner conflict and empower you to mend broken connections, making your bonds with others more authentic and whole.

Reframing Life's Challenges with Joy

Another step in the HeartFaith practice is reframing your perception with joy. Although it's part of the meditation, it functions more like a visualization exercise to set the tone for the day ahead. This involves imagining your day through a lens of happiness and preparing your mind to embrace whatever comes your way with a positive outlook. This step follows after you've reached a place of inner stillness, where you're simply aware of a loving presence. As you dwell in that space of stillness, there inevitably comes a moment when you need to transition back to your daily responsibilities—meetings, tasks, and the everyday situations we all encounter.

To face the day ahead with the right mindset, it's essential to set your attitude intentionally. Often, there's a goal you're working toward—something important you need to accomplish. And inevitably, challenges will arise. While our natural instinct might be to avoid difficulties, much like physical exercise that strengthens our bodies, life's challenges actually present opportunities to build resilience and enhance our overall wellbeing.

Incorporating joy into your meditation practice helps you approach these challenges differently—not as burdens, but as opportunities that shape you and deepen your capacity for mental wellbeing. It's important to understand that happiness is ultimately a natural outflow of peace and love. In that sense, visualizing joy may not be necessary for everyone. When you are continuously aware of a transcendent inner loving presence, happiness follows naturally.

However, even after experiencing deep peace during meditation, it's common for many of us to fall back into familiar habits when confronted with everyday challenges. This is why taking a moment to infuse your meditation with joy—visualizing it as painting your heart with vibrant, joyful colors—can be incredibly impactful. It helps you carry that sense of joy with you, enabling you to approach every moment of the day with a light and joyful countenance.

As you move into this stage, think of happiness as a filter through which you can view your experiences. It's the feeling of contentment that arises not from perfect conditions but from a profound sense of inner peace and connection. Neuroscience shows us that happiness is closely linked to the brain's reward system, which releases neurotransmitters like dopamine, serotonin, and oxytocin —chemicals that help regulate mood, foster social bonds, and create feelings of pleasure. However, from a spiritual perspective, happiness goes beyond the physical—it's a state of being that arises from a deeper connection with your true self and God. As described by mystics like Julian of Norwich and St. John of the Cross, it is the natural outcome of surrendering to divine love.

Now, take a deep breath, allowing yourself to relax into this awareness of happiness. Imagine a challenge you've faced recently or in the past that brought you stress or frustration. Picture it as if you're watching it on a television screen. Observe this experience without judgment—just see it for what it was. Then, shift your perspective. Imagine placing a new screen next to the first, showing the same situation but viewed through the eyes of happiness and joy. Allow yourself to feel how different this experience is when seen through a lens of contentment and gratitude.

Stay in this moment, fully immersed in this new perspective. Visualize handling this challenge with a sense of joy, as if happiness guides you through it. This simple mental shift, repeated during meditation, reprograms your mind and heart to approach life's difficulties not as threats but as pathways to growth and fulfillment. You are training your brain, particularly your subconscious, to perceive life's moments through this uplifting filter, altering how you experience everything that unfolds.

This practice is not about ignoring pain or pretending everything is perfect. It's about recognizing that beneath the surface of every challenge lies an opportunity for joy and growth. Just as the biblical text says, "for the joy set before Him, Jesus endured the cross,"[3] you too can find strength in placing happiness as a guiding light before you. Visualize yourself embracing your day's challenges with this inner happiness, knowing there is good on the other side. Much like the satisfaction of completing a strenuous workout, the joy comes not just from the result but from the journey itself.

As you finish this practice, take a few more deep breaths, holding onto this joy. With consistent meditation, this joyful lens becomes more instinctive, allowing you to face any challenge with a lightness of heart and an unshakeable peace.

A Life of Grace ... A Shift in Identity and Reality

The final step in HeartFaith meditation invites you to envision your life as immersed in grace—an elevated state of being where you experience reality through the lens of a loving presence. Grace here isn't a theological concept. It's a way of living where grace becomes the foundation of who you are, shaping your interactions with others and transforming your perception of the world around you. It's about stepping into divine favor—not as something earned by belonging to a particular group or following specific rules, but as a natural result of aligning with the wisdom, creativity, and flow of the One-Life.

When your sense of self is aligned with grace, you find yourself attuned to the stillness within—the birthplace of all creativity. This inner stillness allows you to engage with life in an effortless way. Solutions, opportunities, and guidance seem to arise naturally as if you're in sync with a higher rhythm. Life begins to unfold with ease, and the right people, ideas, and circumstances appear at just the right time. This isn't mere luck; it's a direct result of living in alignment with the deeper, loving intelligence of the universe.

Grace also transforms how you show up in the world. As your identity shifts, you begin to embody grace in your actions, words, and attitudes. You become more gracious toward others, especially those who have hurt you or let you down. Instead of reacting with anger or resentment, you respond with compassion and understanding, seeing that everyone is navigating their own challenges. Grace allows you to release the need for retribution, let go of grudges, and choose kindness, even when difficult.

This graciousness extends to how you treat yourself. When you make mistakes, you no longer spiral into self-criticism or regret. Instead, you acknowledge your humanity, learn from the experience, and move forward. Grace helps you forgive yourself, offering self-compassion rather than judgment, and keeps you grounded in the present rather than stuck in the past.

Living in grace also means perceiving reality from a higher state of consciousness. You begin to see beyond everyday frustrations, conflicts, and disappointments, tapping into a deeper awareness that recognizes the interconnectedness of all things. From this elevated perspective, challenges become growth opportunities, pain becomes a pathway to greater understanding, and every encounter becomes a chance to express love.

Grace is about flowing with life rather than resisting it. When aligned with grace, you trust the process, even when circumstances don't unfold as expected. You recognize a more extensive intelligence at work and allow yourself to be guided by it. Instead of trying to control every outcome, you engage with life from a place of trust, surrender, and openness, knowing that a loving presence supports you and guides you toward your highest purpose.

Incorporating grace into your daily meditation can reshape your entire human experience, guiding you to live in harmony with the divine flow that elevates your consciousness and enriches your life. This simple practice rewrites your subconscious, infusing it with new instincts of patience, kindness, compassion, and ease.

As you conclude your HeartFaith meditation, take a moment to visualize your typical day playing out on a screen before you—scenes from the past where you might have lost your temper, made mistakes, or felt inadequate. Watch these moments without judgment; simply observe them as they are.

Now, imagine a second screen beside the first, displaying your day transformed by grace. See yourself moving through each moment calmly and confidently, embodying grace in all you do. You respond with patience, extend compassion to yourself and others, and face every challenge with an inner assurance that you are supported. Let this new perspective unfold before you, feeling it wash over you and settle deeply within.

Remain in this space, fully immersed in the experience of living with grace, letting it fill your heart and mind. When practiced consistently, this simple yet transformative shift begins to rewire your brain and reshape your subconscious. You are training yourself to rise into an elevated state of consciousness—a Christ-consciousness—where life flows effortlessly in the fullness of grace, and each moment becomes an opportunity to embody the divine presence.

Let the Transformation Begin

Just as the luthier in our opening story fine-tuned the violin to bring forth its harmonious melodies, HeartFaith meditation offers the tools to fine-tune your inner self, aligning you with the profound rhythms of the Divine. This practice is not just a method; it's a transformative journey that reshapes how you perceive, engage with, and understand the world around you.

At the core of HeartFaith meditation is the shift from intellectual faith to a heart-centered faith. This isn't about adhering to a set of beliefs or narratives; it's about experiencing a deep, authentic connection to God and the universe. It's a faith that resonates with love, peace, and a profound sense of unity with all that exists.

As you weave Gratitude, Peace, Love, Joy, and Grace into your daily meditation, you open yourself to a transformation that transcends the physical and mental. You embark on a spiritual journey that aligns you with your true essence, freeing you from the limitations of the ego and expanding your heart to embrace the all-encompassing One-Life and the Spirit of God.

11

THE WISDOM WITHIN

I magine facing a tough decision at work where the stakes are high, emotions are intense, and the solution isn't immediately apparent. It could be a heated debate with a colleague or a project with far-reaching consequences. In moments like these, knowledge and technical skills, while important, aren't enough. What you truly need is wisdom—the ability to step back, sift through the complexity, understand the different perspectives at play, and manage your own emotions.

Wisdom is often defined as the integration of mental, emotional, and social intelligence that allows us to thoughtfully interpret and respond to challenges. We have all encountered situations where someone, convinced of their superior knowledge and intelligence, made decisions that ultimately proved unwise. To make sagacious decisions, we must also be aware of our own biases and attuned to the thoughts and feelings of others. Wisdom requires us to step back from raw emotions and personal prejudices, gain a broader perspective, and choose actions that serve the greater good, even when not everyone may feel their personal interests are met.

In the Bible, King Solomon is regarded as the wisest man in the world. According to the story, Solomon received wisdom as a divine gift after he asked God for discernment to lead his people, choosing wisdom over wealth or power. One famous account highlighting his wisdom involves two women who came before him, each claiming to be the mother of the same infant. The conflict arose when one woman's baby tragically died, with both women now claiming the surviving child.

In a display of insight, Solomon proposed to resolve the dispute by cutting the baby in half and giving each woman a portion. One woman agreed, but the other, overcome with love and compassion, pleaded to give the child to the other woman rather than see him harmed. Recognizing the true mother's selfless heart, Solomon ordered the child be given to her, demonstrating his ability to discern truth and justice in even the most emotional situation.

Later in Solomon's story, it becomes evident that he did not display the same level of wisdom in his personal life. The Bible tells us that Solomon had 700 wives and 300 concubines. Many of these marriages were politically motivated to secure alliances with other nations. However, these relationships diverted his focus, influenced his decisions, and contributed to Israel's eventual downfall. Solomon's wisdom brought him great wealth, and with wealth came power, which ultimately fed his ego. As his ego grew, it overshadowed his wisdom, leading him away from the discernment that once defined his leadership.

What we learn from Solomon's story is that wisdom is lost when the ego takes control. The ego, which prioritizes self-preservation and self-importance, clouds our judgment, distorts our perception, and can lead even the wisest among us astray. When the ego reigns, wisdom is overshadowed, and the ability to see clearly is compromised. Decisions driven by pride, fear, or the need for validation replace those guided by insight, compassion, and understanding. This shift away from wisdom's light can have far-reaching consequences, as seen in Solomon's eventual downfall.

What Is Wisdom?

At its core, wisdom is more than just acquiring knowledge or having a sharp intellect. Spiritual traditions teach that true wisdom is about accessing a profound, intuitive understanding beyond everyday thinking. An inner knowing—wisdom—emerges when we move beyond the narrow lens of the ego and our self-interests to view life from a broader, interconnected perspective.

The Book of Proverbs poetically depicts wisdom *(hokhmah)* as a female figure who exists alongside God at the foundation of the universe, pouring herself out in love and actively shaping all of creation. She is depicted not just as a distant, abstract force but as a nurturing figure who invites everyone to dine at her table, offering nourishment, healing, and restoration. This portrayal of *hokhmah* emerged during a time of great suffering and captivity for the Jewish people, when the aftermath of wars had left many men dead, and there was a longing for a divine presence that embodied the loving, compassionate qualities of a mother. In this context, *hokhmah* became associated with the Messiah—a redeemer who would gather the people and pour herself out in love.

Scholars and mystics who have delved into the deeper meanings of *hokhmah* by analyzing its letters and linguistic roots reveal a profound connection between wisdom and consciousness. *Hokhmah* was understood as the initial spark of insight and self-awareness that gives rise to all creation, bridging individual consciousness with the divine source. This wisdom was seen not just as knowledge but as "*koach mah*," or "the power of selflessness," emphasizing the surrender of the ego and merging one's sense of self with the greater, unified consciousness of God.[1] In this mystical view, individual consciousness is not separate but is a reflection of the one ultimate consciousness—the divine "I am" that underlies all reality.

Early Christian thought also embraced this connection, linking *hokhmah* with the concept of *logos* as described in the Gospel of John. Here, wisdom is not just an abstract principle but is made manifest in Christ, embodying

God's self-awareness in human form. Christ represents the ultimate expression of wisdom, transcending personal ego and revealing the oneness of all existence. In this view, Jesus's awareness of his divine identity as Christ was a recognition that the individual "I" within his human form was one with the sacred "I Am that I Am." Thus, in Jesus, the wisdom present at the beginning of creation was fully expressed in human form, mirroring the divine source of life through the lens of love, unity, and self-lessness.

Throughout this book, we've explored a profound theme often missed in traditional Christianity: the under-standing that the Messiah, or Christ, as seen by mystics, is not limited to a historical Jesus alone. The idea of the "Christ in us" or the universal Christ had been hidden throughout the ages, but through the archetype of Jesus, it has been revealed to those who awaken to this deeper reality. As we discussed earlier, this is what Jesus referred to as the kingdom of God within us. The divine "I can," or the intelligence that permeates the universe, flows through consciousness—it is within us, around us, and omnipresent. When we return to the Beginning—to a place of inner stillness—we glimpse the kingdom of God and step into a realm of infinite wisdom.

This is more than just a spiritual insight; it parallels concepts in quantum physics that suggest everything is interconnected at the deepest level. Theories like quantum entanglement and the unified field propose that the separateness we perceive is an illusion and that consciousness is not merely a byproduct of brain activity but the fundamental essence that underpins all reality.

What does this mean for us today? Simply put, true wisdom emerges when we quiet our minds and connect with inner stillness, allowing us to view life beyond the ego. This inner alignment becomes the source of our well-being, reshaping how we think and perceive reality. Our minds are renewed, and qualities like patience, nonjudgment, confidence, forgiveness, and creativity become central to how we experience life. These qualities transform our interactions with others, leading to a more fulfilling life and possibly a more harmonious world. Let's explore how these qualities shape how we face challenges.

The Wisdom of Patience

From my earliest memories, I have felt a deep sense of urgency. Growing up believing that the Gospel had to be spread before the prophesied end times, I lived with a restless drive. After high school in Sweden, I moved to Canada, enrolling in Bible college with a clear plan: complete my studies and then hit the mission field before the looming tribulation arrived. It felt like a race against time, with every moment overshadowed by the pressure of what was coming next.

This impatience seeped into every aspect of my life. Whether hurrying through traffic behind the wheel or rushing through aisles at the store, I was perpetually fixated on reaching the next goal, the next task, the next place to be. Each day felt like a ticking clock, and the present moment never seemed enough.

After my profound meditation experience in 2006, a slow transformation began. Spending more time meditating, I noticed how many of my long-held beliefs started dissolving. I realized that spirituality was not about possessing superior beliefs, as the ego might have suggested, but about an inner awakening to a harmonious oneness with God and all creation. Along with this deepened sense of presence came a sharpened awareness of the impatience that had run through my life. Even with greater mental wellbeing, restlessness lingered, diminishing but never fully disappearing.

One day, I was in my car, my frustration building as a slow driver caused me to miss a green light. Impatience initially swelled within me, but then, in a moment, something shifted. A gentle but powerful thought washed over me: Why am I rushing? What awaited me that was truly more valuable than the present moment?

As I sat there waiting for the light to turn green again, I became completely present, observing the person crossing the street and even feeling a connection with them as they struggled to get across. For that one minute at the traffic light, and as I continued my journey home, I observed everything around me—the trees swaying gently in the breeze, the sunlight reflecting off car windows, and the rhythmic hum of life moving all around. I was filled with a deep sense of awe at the aliveness of everything I observed. It was as if, in slowing down, I had awakened to a richness that had been there all along, waiting for me to notice.

This revelation taught me that patience is a gateway to a deeper experience of life and an expression of wisdom itself. When we are patient, we open our hearts to the present moment, seeing it not as an obstacle to overcome but as a gift to be cherished. It transforms our restless urgency into a calm presence, our hurried thoughts into mindful awareness, and every ordinary moment into a sacred experience.

Studies show that cultivating patience can significantly impact our physiological and psychological wellbeing. Our heart rhythms become more coherent when we are patient, balancing the sympathetic and parasympathetic nervous systems. This harmony helps reduce stress, lower heart rates, and create a state of calm that allows us to respond to life's challenges gracefully. This physiological shift enhances our access to wisdom, helping us approach life's complexities with a clearer, more thoughtful mind.

So, when you find yourself caught in impatience or frustration, take a moment to pause. Let go of the urge to rush, to control every situation, and to push forward. Connect with the stillness within you, and allow patience to settle over your thoughts and actions. In this space, you'll discover that what you've been seeking is not out there in the next accomplishment or milestone but in the gentle unfolding of each moment.

The Wisdom of Being Nonjudgmental

The ego-driven mind naturally tends to impulsively cast judgments about ourselves and others. These judgments can spring up in numerous everyday situations. For instance, when someone cuts us off in traffic, a colleague underperforms, or we're unable to spend enough time with our children, our minds might automatically start forming judgments about the circumstances in which we find ourselves.

Even when we meet someone for the first time, we often make immediate assessments about that person based on superficial attributes like appearance, clothing, gender, race, perceived wealth, profession, nationality, fame, or even the type of jewelry they wear. However, these judgments often reveal more about us than the individuals we judge. Driven by a need to feel unique or superior, the ego swiftly decides whether a person will bolster our self-image. This decision is influenced by the narrative in which the mind is currently absorbed, be it heroism, self-pity, or guilt. Hence, our judgment of another person is less about objective facts and more about our subjective interpretation of those facts, often colored by biases that reinforce the ego.

For example, if you meet someone you deem attractive and they show interest in you, it boosts your self-esteem, leading you to form a favorable opinion of them. Conversely, if that person seems disinterested, your sense of self is threatened, prompting you to subconsciously look for faults in them to criticize. This pattern of judgment, rooted in how others affect our sense of self, highlights the ego's influence on our perceptions and interactions.

Another common way we judge others is by categorizing them and assigning labels. For example, if we heavily identify with our job, we might habitually ask someone we've just met, "What do you do?" This question isn't just small talk. Subconsciously, we assess whether their occupation places them above or below us in our perceived social hierarchy. Similarly, if our self-worth is closely tied to our political beliefs, we might try to figure out if a new acquaintance leans conservative or liberal. If their views differ, we might automatically feel more enlightened, boosting our ego.

These prejudiced judgments, whether directed at ourselves or others, always stem from the egoic mind, which views relationships through a lens of either superiority or inferiority. When we encounter someone whom we perceive as more important or successful than ourselves, we choose to associate with them, as if their significance will reflect positively on us. Conversely, suppose such individuals reject or distance themselves from us. In that case, our reaction is often to discredit or disparage them to inflate our sense of worth and respectability.

The tendency of our minds to judge others and ourselves is a significant source of suffering. When we judge and condemn, we block the flow of wisdom within us. The ego takes over, distorting our view and keeping us from acting in ways that foster healing and wholeness. Instead of focusing on the greater good, we prioritize our own desires, which ultimately drive us apart and turn others into adversaries. True wisdom, however, sees the bigger picture—it unites people and restores broken relationships.

We naturally become less judgmental when we connect with our deepest self—the pure, unconditioned consciousness. Early Christian writings describe this as the mind of Christ. As Paul wrote, in this state, divisions disappear: There is no Gentile or Jew, slave or free, male or female. Everything is seen as an expression of Christ. To condemn another is, in essence, to condemn Christ and ourselves, for we are all one in this universal Christ.

As we align more deeply with this inner presence, we begin to accept both our own imperfections and the differences we see in others. Concerns about how we are perceived fade, and we discover common ground with those who may seem different. In this space, a deeper wisdom arises, bringing forth solutions that not only benefit us but also extend goodness to those around us.

The Wisdom of Forgiveness

Nurturing an awareness of presence can infuse your days with wonder, peace, and love. This spiritual awakening enriches your relationships, improves your health, and brings newfound clarity and calm to your professional life. Yet, you might still face moments that stir up deep-rooted resentment and anger. Life's minor frustrations, like being cut off in traffic or hearing an offhand negative remark, can be forgiven and forgotten relatively easily. However, deeper wounds—the pain of mistreatment, betrayal, or rejection from someone dear—pose a real challenge. These profound hurts can lead to significant inner turmoil, making forgiveness feel like an uphill battle and tempting us to subconsciously bury painful experiences rather than confront them with wisdom.

However, this act of suppression does not eliminate the hurt. Instead, it allows resentment to grow—a persistent bitterness that lingers, stemming from actual or perceived injustices. This resentment can manifest as ongoing anger toward those who have wronged us, or even toward ourselves, marked by an inability to release past grievances. Such inner turmoil weighs heavily on the heart and mind, blocking the flow of wisdom.

In these moments, it's essential to recognize the power of forgiveness as a gateway to inner wisdom. Forgiveness is more than just pardoning others—it's a healing process that frees the heart from the burden of past pain. It's important to remember that forgiveness is rarely instant; it's often a gradual and evolving journey.

In my own experience, as I awakened to a more profound sense of presence, I found that many grievances naturally faded away. However, there were still moments when feelings of resentment and bitterness would resurface. During meditation, I allowed these emotions to arise, observing them without judgment and creating a sense of distance between my awareness and the feelings. Over time, I realized these emotions were not a reflection of my true self, but echoes of old conditioned responses of my mind.

Occasionally, during meditation, old buried memories—the deeper roots of my lingering resentment—would resurface. I began to recognize the unconscious patterns etched into my subconscious, patterns that had shaped my reactions and created the triggers for those feelings of bitterness. By allowing these early memories to emerge within a space of love, forgiveness, and nonjudgment, I could feel the past's tight grip gradually loosen. As this release occurred, forgiveness naturally flowed into other areas of my life, clearing away any lingering bitterness and opening the door to deeper wisdom and healing.

So, what is true forgiveness? It goes beyond simply saying the words, "I forgive you." Genuine forgiveness stems from a deep awareness of our shared connection with those who have wronged us. It echoes Jesus's powerful words on the cross: "Father, forgive them, for they know not what they do." In this prayer, Jesus revealed a profound wisdom —he looked beyond the terrible act committed against him and recognized his inherent unity with the perpetrators. He understood that his oppressors were blinded by their egos, unaware of the divine presence within them. No wonder his response was one of compassion and forgiveness. He recognized that their actions were not a reflection of their true self but of an ego-driven self that didn't know any better.

We learn from Jesus that true forgiveness involves acknowledging that condemning another is, in essence, condemning ourselves and the divine spirit that under-girds all creation. It's not about excusing harmful actions but seeing a more profound reality—the kingdom of God that connects us all. By embracing forgiveness, we step into a dimension where the weight of resentment loses its power over us. Resentment may have taken a toll on our health and wellbeing, but forgiveness sets us free. It opens our hearts to peace, allowing wisdom to guide our thoughts and actions.

Forgiveness isn't just about releasing others from our judgment; it also means releasing ourselves. Many of us carry the weight of regrets—for mistakes we've made, for falling short of our expectations, or for moments when we wish we had acted differently. These regrets can become a constant, heavy burden. But just as we are called to forgive those who hurt us, we are also called to forgive ourselves. This is where practices like HeartFaith meditation come in, helping us to shift our focus to the present moment and connect with the deeper presence. In this stillness, we begin to experience a profound compassion, allowing the process of self-forgiveness to unfold.

Holding onto resentment for our own mistakes builds invisible walls around our hearts, preventing true healing and growth. Guilt, shame, or feelings of unworthiness can quietly persist, robbing us of life's fullness. But through HeartFaith meditation, we learn to meet these emotions with gentleness rather than judgment. We come to understand that our past actions, no matter how flawed, do not define who we truly are. As we dismantle negative thought patterns, our potential is no longer hindered, sharpening our ability to navigate life with clarity, kindness, and creativity. By releasing these burdens, we tap into a deeper awareness that guides us to approach each moment with grace and wisdom.

How Wisdom Unlocks Creativity

When we live with wisdom, we tap into a deeper flow of insight and inspiration, and this is where creativity truly blossoms. Creativity, at its heart, isn't just about making art. It's about seeing new possibilities, recognizing patterns where others may not, and bringing something fresh and meaningful into existence. Whether finding a solution to a work problem, coming up with an innovative business idea, or figuring out how to navigate a tricky family situation, creativity shows up in countless areas of our lives.

But creativity is not something that can be forced. New insights, solutions to problems, and innovative ideas tend to emerge when we cultivate a sense of inner stillness. By stepping back from the constant hustle and allowing room for things to unfold without rushing toward a conclusion, creativity flows more naturally.

In today's fast-paced world, creativity can easily be stifled as everything pushes us toward speed and productivity. When we are focused on meeting deadlines or increasing output, we rarely give ourselves the breathing room necessary for new ideas to form. But wisdom reminds us to stay present, let go of ego, and rest in the stillness of our true self. When we nurture this stillness, creativity often surprises us with fresh, unexpected solutions that would have otherwise remained hidden.

Openness to new ideas is another key to creativity. To be creative, we must be willing to explore the unknown, take risks, and let go of the fear of failure. But that's easier said than done, right? One of the biggest roadblocks to creativity is our inner critic—the one that wants to judge every idea before it's even had a chance to breathe. Too often, we're quick to label our thoughts as "good" or "bad," "worthwhile" or "useless," and in doing so, we shut down the creative process before it even starts.

This is where wisdom can help us again. When we let go of judgment and approach life with curiosity, we give our ideas space to grow. Wisdom teaches us that even unconventional or strange ideas can be the stepping stones to something greater. By suspending judgment, we create the mental space needed for creativity to flourish—without all the limitations that usually come with our preconceived notions or fears of not being good enough.

When wisdom and creativity come together, the results can be truly transformative—not just for us personally but also for how we contribute to the world around us. Here are just a few of the many benefits creativity brings:

Problem Solving and Innovation. Creativity is at the heart of problem solving. It allows us to approach challenges from new angles and find solutions that might not be immediately obvious. Whether in business, science, or everyday life, creative thinking enables us to break free from conventional patterns and develop innovative approaches to our obstacles.

Personal Growth and Fulfillment. Creativity is deeply tied to self-expression and personal fulfillment. When we engage in creative activities, whether writing, painting, cooking, or brainstorming new ideas, we tap into a sense of purpose and joy. Creativity helps us express our deepest thoughts, emotions, and perspectives, allowing us to connect profoundly with others and ourselves. And when we create from a place of wisdom, our creativity is not driven by ego or the need for approval, but by an authentic desire to contribute something meaningful to the world.

Improved Mental Wellbeing. Engaging in creative activities has been shown to reduce stress, increase happiness, and improve overall mental health. Creativity helps us process emotions, release tension, and connect with a sense of flow, where time seems to disappear, and we are fully absorbed in the present moment.

Building Stronger Connections with Others. Creativity also plays a crucial role in building empathy and connection.

When we engage in creative activities, whether through art, storytelling, or innovation, we share our perspectives and experiences with others, creating bridges of understanding and compassion. Wisdom deepens this by reminding us of the interconnectedness of all people and the importance of expressing our shared humanity through creative endeavors.

Embracing a Life of Wisdom

In this chapter, we've explored how the deeper wisdom of the universe unfolds through patience, non-judgment, and forgiveness—qualities that open us to a life of greater insight and clarity. We've also considered how wisdom fuels creativity, allowing us to solve problems, approach challenges, and view the world with fresh eyes. At the heart of these qualities is a deeper awareness of inner presence, the foundation of a wise and creative mind.

As you practice HeartFaith meditation and become more attuned to this loving presence, you'll notice a profound shift in how your mind operates. You'll begin to move away from the reactive patterns of the ego and instead see life through a broader, more expansive lens of unity. This awakening empowers you to navigate daily challenges with both wisdom and creativity.

Decisions at work, choices about your health, and interactions with loved ones or others you encounter throughout your day will no longer be driven by impulse or fear. Instead, you'll respond with a wisdom that flows with grace and creativity, revealing beauty and meaning in even the smallest moments. Each day becomes a canvas, waiting to be filled with wise, compassionate, and creative strokes that enhance your personal wellbeing and contribute to our shared, collective wellbeing.

12

A LIFE OF AWE

I t was about 4:20 a.m. when a beep from a fridge's ajar door unexpectedly woke me. I rubbed my eyes, stood up, and groggily navigated my way to the kitchen in the dark. As I passed through the living room, I noticed a supermoon shining through the large windows, illuminating the winter night sky. Its light was mirrored by the surface of the backyard pool, creating a captivating image—it was as if there were two moons, one suspended in the sky and the other floating in the water.

Mesmerized by the wonder of the moment, I stepped outside and stood in awe, utterly present. There was no sound, no distractions, only outer silence and pure inner stillness as I beheld this extraordinary sight.

This wasn't the first time I had experienced such a profound sense of awe. Since my youth, I've had moments when I felt the presence of something vast, a force that transcended my understanding, something shrouded in mystery and imbued with a sense of the sacred. I recall countless times of standing under the vast canopy of the night sky, gazing at stars that dotted the cosmic expanse, their light piercing the enveloping darkness—each star a reminder of the universe's incomprehensible vastness.

Undoubtedly, you too have experienced these singular moments of awe that linger in your memory like precious gems. You may recall standing at the ocean's edge as the sun dips below the horizon, the sky painted in vibrant orange, pink, and purple hues. The world around you falls silent, save for the gentle lapping of waves against the shore. In that calm majesty, you feel a deep connection to something far greater than yourself and a profound sense of peace enveloping your being.

Or you might think back to the first time you held a newborn child, the weight of their tiny body in your arms, the delicate features of their face, and the innocent gaze meeting yours. In that moment, time stands still. You are holding a new life, a miracle in its truest form, and it's an overwhelming realization of love and responsibility that words can hardly capture.

Maybe your moment of awe was found in the embrace of nature—a walk through a lush forest, the canopy over-head dappled with sunlight, the air rich with the scent of earth and leaves. As you walk, the noise of the modern world fades away, replaced by the symphony of rustling leaves, chirping birds, and the wind's gentle whisper.

There, amidst the grandeur of nature, you encounter a profound mystery, an unspoken understanding of life's interconnectedness and the beauty of existence.

These moments of awe are universal, yet deeply personal. They remind us of our place in the intricate mosaic of life. They are instances where the ordinary world fades, and we are left face-to-face with the extraordinary, feeling both humbled and elevated by the experience. These moments stay with us, shaping our perception of the world and our place within it.

What if these moments of awe could transform into a perpetual life of awe? Imagine living in a state of awareness of something vast and mysterious, beyond the grasp of our minds—a profound realization of our unity with the transcending presence that underpins all reality: God. Envision a life where awe isn't reserved for just the extraordinary moments that sporadically appear but is woven into the fabric of our everyday consciousness, even in moments that might initially seem mundane.

Imagine experiencing this awe as you wake up and savor your first cup of coffee in the morning, immersing yourself in the simple joy of being alive. Consider the wonder when you observe your son, daughter, or dog relishing their breakfast, and you feel an overwhelming sense of love because you are fully present with them. Imagine feeling this awe as you drive to work or school and encounter a stranger, recognizing a profound sense of unity that transcends physical limitations.

Awe does not need to be confined to those rare moments when we face something majestic. Instead, awe is about being conscious of the vibrancy and essence of life itself. It's about recognizing each moment as a precious gift, surpassing all the material wealth, fame, and power the world can offer. It's about being acutely aware that, as the Bible says, "Christ is all and in all"—finding the divine in every aspect of our existence.

If we distill the essence of this book into a single, defining word, few words would be more fitting than "awe." Throughout this book, we've navigated a myriad of concepts designed to guide us toward inner wholeness and freedom. Yet, few words embody the life we are destined to live better than awe.

So, let us ponder—What is this awe? How can we integrate this deep awareness of awe into our everyday lives, thereby nurturing a state of inner peace and a profound love for the entirety of life? Moreover, how can we utilize our talents and innovative thinking to create moments that evoke awe in others, illuminating the world with greater light and wonder?

This chapter delves into these questions, inviting you to understand awe and experience it even in the most ordinary aspects of life. It's about transforming awe from an occasional marvel into a daily, living reality, where each moment invites us to connect with the profound beauty and mystery of our existence.

Defining Awe

In the lingering hours following my pre-dawn experience in the backyard, a realization dawned on me as I
sat in quiet reflection. Had my morning unfolded just
slightly differently—waking a moment later, reaching
instinctively for my iPhone to sift through the news—the
miraculous moonlit spectacle would have unfolded
unseen by me, its marvel unnoticed, as if it never
existed.

The supermoon, in all its nocturnal glory, would have
continued its celestial dance, casting silver reflections
upon the still waters of my pool. This ethereal scene, a
confluence of cosmic timing and nature's serenity, might
have been just another secret of the universe, quietly
playing out in my backyard, hidden in plain sight. Such
phenomena, requiring the confluence of a supermoon,
the stillness of the night, and a cloudless sky, had likely
graced my residence numerous times in the past, yet
remained veiled from my awareness.

But there I was, standing outside at 4:20 a.m., enveloped in
a series of profound experiences. The moon and its
mirrored image on the water's surface captivated me,
ushering me into a state of complete presence. The usual
preoccupations of the day and the reason behind my early
awakening were forgotten for a fleeting moment. I was
immersed in a state of inner stillness, or what we might
call pure consciousness. This state birthed deep awe,
characterized by an overwhelming sense of encountering

something vast that transcended the essence of my existence.

This awe was not merely a reaction to the stunning beauty before me that morning. It was also an awakening, an awareness of life itself, that eluded the grasp of logic and language. Had my mind been clouded with lingering thoughts of the previous night or the day ahead, this feeling of awe would have remained elusive. Awe, as I experienced it, was a response to the enigmatic mystery of life, manifesting in this present moment of inner stillness.

As I pondered further on the nature of awe, I recalled the many instances during meditation when a deep peace and love enveloped me, always accompanied by this same sense of awe. In those instances, I felt an indescribable inner aliveness, leaving me in the reverent wonder of something far larger than myself—an experience akin to what the Epicurean poets described as "in God, we live, and move, and have our being."

From these reflections, I've come to understand that at any given moment, we can pause, become fully present, and tune in to the very essence of life. This might happen as we watch the delicate dance of leaves in a gentle breeze, each movement a quiet symphony of nature's grace. Or perhaps it's in the unguarded laughter of a child, a sound so pure and uninhibited that it invites us into a moment of joyful simplicity. It could even be during a mundane activity like washing dishes, where the sensation of warm water and the rhythmic motion of our hands become a meditative experience, connecting us to the simple, yet profound act of being.

These seemingly ordinary instances hold within them the potential for extraordinary revelation. They are opportunities to witness the intricate beauty of existence and to feel the pulse of life in all things. In such moments, when we allow ourselves to be fully immersed in the now, we transcend the habitual rush of thoughts and worries.

In doing so, we open ourselves to an experience of sacred awe and wonder, an intimate encounter with the profound mysteries of existence. Every breath becomes a gateway to the infinite, where each heartbeat resonates with the timeless rhythm of the universe, and the ordinary unfurls into the extraordinary. Such is the power of presence, the key to unlocking a life filled with awe and profound connection to the world around us.

Moving Beyond the Egoic Self to Awaken to Your True Self

Across the expanse of history, there are moments when awe has redefined human perception, transcending the narrow confines of the egoic self and pointing toward a universal essence of love that binds all reality. These instances of awe reveal a profound truth: We are part of something far more significant than our individual selves, a truth powerfully demonstrated in the lives and works of mystics like Julian of Norwich and Margaret Fuller.

Julian of Norwich, a Christian mystic from the fourteenth and fifteenth centuries, captured this in her *Revelations of Divine Love.* Her profound encounters with the love of Christ, born out of illness and suffering, opened her to an understanding of love that was vast, unconditional, and all-encompassing. Julian's experiences transcended mere emotional responses, becoming transformative experiences that reshaped her perception of both God and the world. Her renowned affirmation, "All shall be well, and all shall be well, and all manner of thing shall be well," resonates as a testament to this profound awe and love.[1]

Similarly, Margaret Fuller, a pivotal figure in the women's rights movement of the nineteenth century, experienced awe that transcended the egoic self. In her seminal work, *Woman in the Nineteenth Century,* she envisioned humanity reaching its full potential in a state deeply rooted in divine love. Fuller's awe, sparked in a church and fully realized in nature, was not just a reaction to beauty. It was a profound spiritual awakening that dissolved her egocentric self, connecting her to a larger existence.

Fuller's insight, "*I saw there was no self...that it was only because I thought self as real that I suffered,*" aligns with spiritual teachings that identify the illusion of a separate, ego-driven self as the root of human pain. Her awe was a transformative force, leading to a genuine, unfiltered experience of reality.

The transformative power of awe is further elucidated by scientific studies that show how experiencing awe quiets brain regions associated with the ego, such as self-criticism, anxiety, and depression. Awe shifts us from a self-centered mindset to the realization of being part of a more extensive web of interdependent beings.

This understanding is echoed in the reflections of many astronauts who saw Earth as a cohesive, living entity from the unique vantage point of space, emphasizing our interconnectedness and collective responsibility. In the words of the Canadian Astronaut Chris Hadfield: "To see the Earth from space is to see yourself as part of something bigger. A species that has only just begun to understand its own world and its place in the universe."[2]

Nicole Stott, NASA Astronaut, adds: "It's hard to articulate the impact of seeing Earth from space. It's this beautiful, glowing oasis—a living, breathing organism that we are all a part of. It's a feeling of interconnectedness with all of it and a humbling sense of responsibility to take care of it."[3]

With his profound grasp of the universe, Albert Einstein also articulated this: "A human being is a part of the whole, called by us 'Universe,' a part limited in time and space. He experiences himself, his thoughts, and feelings as something separated from the rest—a kind of optical delusion of his consciousness."[4]

Thus, awe is more than a fleeting sensation. It is a gateway to understanding our proper place in the universe. It dissolves the ego, peels back superficial layers of identity, and deepens our understanding of our role in the grand narrative of life. It's an invitation to recognize that love, in its most universal form, is the foundation of all existence, a unifying force that transcends individual selves and binds us in a shared journey of existence.

The Catalyst for Open-Mindedness and Curiosity

Experiencing awe can fundamentally change the way we think and perceive the world. It fosters mental openness, ignites our curiosity, and encourages us to embrace mystery and the unknown. This profound sense of wonder not only enhances our appreciation for life's intricacies but also propels us toward greater openness to new ideas, the unexplainable, and the strengths and virtues of others.

In essence, awe nurtures a mindset akin to a scientist's—one marked by inquiry, exploration, and a quest for understanding. This shift in perspective can be seen in the stories of some of history's greatest scientific minds, whose moments of awe led to groundbreaking discoveries.

Consider the legendary tale of Isaac Newton and the falling apple. This simple, awe-inspiring moment under an apple tree sparked a profound curiosity in Newton. He pondered why the apple fell straight down and not in any other direction. This curiosity, born from awe, led him to formulate the law of universal gravitation, forever changing our understanding of physics.

Similarly, Galileo Galilei's awe of the night sky led him to significant astronomical discoveries. His use of a telescope to explore the heavens revealed the moons of Jupiter, the phases of Venus, and the rings of Saturn. His awe and curiosity challenged the prevailing views of the universe and expanded our cosmic perspective.

Albert Einstein's awe and curiosity about the nature of light and time led to the development of his theory of special relativity. Imagining himself traveling alongside a beam of light, Einstein wondered about the workings of the universe, leading to revolutionary insights about space and time.

These examples demonstrate that awe does more than just amaze us. It expands our mental horizons. It pushes us to think beyond our existing ideas and understandings, making us more receptive to new ideas and perspectives. In a state of awe, we are more inclined to question, delve deeper into the mysteries of life, and integrate these vast mysteries into more complex systems of understanding.

At its core, awe deepens our connection to the spiritual and transcendent aspects of existence, drawing us closer to a profound understanding of God, love, and the universal wisdom that forms the foundation of all reality. This connection isn't about adhering more rigidly to religious doctrines or clinging to specific beliefs about the nature of the world or its creation. Instead, awe inspires a scientifically open and flexible mindset that seeks more profound understanding and knowledge. It compels us to peer beyond superficial appearances, engage with the expansive systems of life, and appreciate our humble but meaningful place within the grand scheme of things.

Cultivating a Life of Awe through Daily Practices

Living a life imbued with awe isn't just about waiting for extraordinary moments. It's about nurturing a consistent awareness of the beauty and aliveness in everything around us. By integrating HeartFaith meditation and consciously dedicating moments each day to recognize the wonder of life, we can deepen our connection to the world and our deepest self.

HeartFaith meditation is a powerful tool for fostering a life of awe. These meditations encourage us to connect with an inner loving presence, the spirit within that resonates with everything around us. By regularly engaging in these meditations, we cultivate a sense of peace and unity, perceiving "Christ is all and in all"—a phrase that speaks of seeing God in every aspect of creation.

Another practice that I found incredibly helpful is allocating five to ten moments daily to pause and appreciate the beauty of life, which can profoundly shift our perception. These moments could include:

Nature Walks: While walking in nature, pay close attention to the sights, sounds, and smells around you. Observe the intricate patterns of leaves, the gentle sway of trees in the wind, or the harmonious sounds of birds. Let yourself be fully present in this experience, feeling a deep connection to the earth and life itself.

Observing People: Take time to observe people around you —not with judgment, but with appreciation and gratitude. Recognize the unique life story each person carries. This practice helps you see beyond superficial differences, fostering a sense of oneness with humanity.

Art and Music: Engaging with art and music can also be a source of awe. Allow yourself to be fully absorbed in these experiences, noticing the feelings they evoke.

Breath Awareness: Simply focusing on your breath for a few moments can be a powerful way to center yourself and appreciate the vital force of life within you.

Mindful Activities: Whether drinking coffee or walking to your car, immerse yourself fully in the activity. Notice the sensations, the smells, the taste, or the movement. Each of these moments is an opportunity to connect with the aliveness of the present moment.

Reflection and Gratitude: Reflect on the day's events, even the mundane ones, and find elements of awe and gratitude. This could include appreciating a meal, the comfort of your home, or a conversation with a friend.

Recording Your Experiences: Keeping a journal of these moments of awe can enhance this practice's effectiveness. Each day, spend a few minutes writing down your experiences of awe and the feelings associated with them. This record will help you track your journey and deepen your appreciation for these moments.

By committing to these practices, we open ourselves to the wonders that life offers daily. This consistent awareness of the beauty and sacredness in the ordinary leads us to a richer, more fulfilling experience of existence. As we cultivate this life of awe, we find ourselves more aligned with love, compassion, and a profound understanding of our interconnectedness with all things.

Creating a Legacy of Wonder

As we embrace a life of awe, we contribute to a shift in the collective consciousness of our planet. This transformation transcends the mere exchange of beliefs or ideas. It stems from an inner awakening that reaches beyond our thoughts. This profound change cannot be mandated or taught as a belief system. Instead, it's the heart's energy emanating from a spirit in harmony with life. This energy of love radiates naturally when we are fully present and attuned to the awe and wonder of life.

Our purpose becomes clear in this state of being: to use our unique abilities, talents, and gifts to craft moments that awaken others to the awe of life. It's not about inspiring awe in our capabilities but about kindling an awareness of presence, of Love, of God, and of the inter-connectedness of all things.

For instance, if your passion lies in cooking, let your culinary creations become a medium for people to pause in awe, to feel gratitude and connection to the wonder of life. As a designer, you can create spaces that transcend the mundane, inviting people to connect with the beauty and goodness of life. Artists can use their brush to paint canvases that draw viewers into the present moment, allowing them to sense something far larger than themselves.

Regardless of your talents, your mission is to leave a legacy of wonder—to create experiences that allow others to encounter moments of profound awe. Whether you're a teacher shaping young minds with the magic of knowledge, a musician composing melodies that stir the soul, or a gardener nurturing beauty and sustenance from the earth, each role has the power to evoke awe. These experiences, crafted through your unique abilities, can become gateways for others to connect with something larger than themselves and to feel a part of the interconnected web of life. Your legacy of wonder thus becomes a catalyst for others to discover the divine presence within and around them, encouraging a life lived in awe of every unfolding moment.

As a spiritual teacher, I am acutely aware of my limitations. Yet, my deepest hope is that my words, whether spoken or written, might inspire someone to pause in awe, to recognize the beauty of life and the divine presence that underlies all creation—a presence filled with peace, love, and grace.

In this journey, I see Jesus as the exemplar of a life of awe. Jesus taught that his words were spirit and life. They weren't doctrinal statements but carried an energy that transcended the intellect and touched the spirit. His presence and words were so life-giving that they brought healing.

Yet, he always credited people's faith—their awakening to the divine dimension within them—for their healing. In their encounter with Jesus, even if just for a moment, people tapped into that aspect of themselves that was in union with the divine presence. This was true faith, as it moved them beyond mere thoughts and beliefs into a realm of spiritual awareness, where healing was a natural consequence.

Our path forward is not so much about converting others to our beliefs as about awakening to the *loving presence* within us. From this Christ-consciousness sprouts love, joy, peace, and kindness—qualities that can bypass intellectual barriers and touch the very spirit of those around us. Our stories, ideas, and beliefs are mere signposts, guiding us and others to that inner dimension. In embracing a life of awe, we open ourselves and others to the profound beauty and mystery of existence, creating a legacy of wonder that transcends time and space.

EPILOGUE

I once read a story about Desmond Doss, a combat medic during World War II. Standing on the edge of the battlefield at Okinawa, surrounded by the chaos of war, Doss did something extraordinary. While explosions shook the ground and bullets tore through the air, mingling with the cries of wounded men, Doss remained calm—centered in the deep conviction that love and compassion were more powerful forces than the destruction unfolding around him.

Doss had made a promise long before he stepped foot on the battlefield. He believed in the sanctity of life and refused to carry a weapon or take another's life, even in war. This decision, rooted in an unshakable belief in the power of love, confused and even angered his fellow soldiers. Some called him a coward, while others openly mocked him.

When his battalion was ordered to take the Maeda Escarpment, a 400-foot sheer cliff known as Hacksaw Ridge, they were met with fierce resistance. Enemy soldiers were hidden in the hills, and every step forward was met with relentless gunfire and explosions. The battlefield was a scene of unimaginable destruction, as men fell one after another under the heavy barrage of fire.

Many soldiers retreated, desperate to escape the deadly onslaught. But Doss stayed. Armed only with his faith and his compassion, he moved toward the injured, his heart attuned to their suffering. He had no weapon, but he knew the power of love that radiated from within could transcend the violence around him. With each step, he silently prayed for strength, asking, "Help me save just one more."

One by one, Doss carried soldiers to the edge of the cliff. His body strained under the weight of their brokenness, but his heart never wavered. As he lowered each man down the ridge using nothing more than a rope and his bare hands, Doss felt a deep, inner connection with something larger than himself—a presence that guided him through every act of love, even amidst the chaos of war.

In that moment, Doss embodied what it means to live from the higher consciousness. His actions weren't driven by a sense of duty or fear, but by the profound awareness that every life held sacred worth. It didn't matter that these were the same men who had ridiculed him or doubted his beliefs. Doss saw beyond their judgments and into the shared humanity that connected them all.

Each time he returned to the battlefield, his body was weakened from the wounds and exhaustion, but his spirit was fortified by the quiet power within him. Seventy-five times he repeated the same prayer: "Help me get just one more." Seventy-five lives were saved because Doss chose to act from love rather than fear.

What makes Desmond Doss's story extraordinary is not just the number of lives he saved, but the consciousness from which he operated. While the world around him was consumed by violence, Doss tapped into a different reality —a reality where love, courage, and compassion flow effortlessly from the stillness of inner peace. In doing so, he demonstrated that even in the most hostile of environments, love can be the greatest force for healing and transformation.

By the end of the battle, Doss's fellow soldiers no longer mocked him. They stood in awe of the power that flowed through him—the quiet, unassuming force of unconditional love that had saved them.

In recognition of his courage, Desmond Doss became the first conscientious objector to receive the Medal of Honor. But for Doss, the true victory wasn't in the medal or the recognition. It was in knowing that he had lived from the heart, from the place where love is infinite, fearless, and unconditionally given. His life was a testimony to the truth that when we awaken to the power of love within us, there is no limit to what we can achieve—even in the midst of the greatest trials.

The story of Desmond Doss illustrates the power of living from a place of love, even in the face of unimaginable adversity. His courage was rooted not in a desire to prove himself, but in the deep conviction that love is stronger than fear—a love that transcends the ego's demands and allows the heart to be guided by something greater than himself.

In much the same way, the Lovingkindness Meditation, which concludes this book, invites us to connect with that same depth of presence within. It's a practice that fosters compassion, understanding, and forgiveness—qualities that align us with the same consciousness from which Doss operated. While the battlefield we face today may not involve physical warfare, the emotional and mental battles we encounter in our relationships and daily lives often leave us wounded, weighed down by resentment, judgment, or unforgiveness.

But like Doss, we have the opportunity to choose love in these moments. This is why I am closing with this meditation that has been especially meaningful to me. Lovingkindness Meditation offers a practical way to experience the ascending life more deeply. Through this practice, love flows not only to ourselves but also to others— even those we find difficult to forgive. In doing so, we create a ripple effect that can transform both our inner world and the world around us.

Here's how the Lovingkindness Meditation unfolds...

Seek out a quiet spot where you won't be disturbed. Sit comfortably in an upright position on a chair or the ground. Avoid lying down to maintain alertness throughout the meditation.

Gently close your eyes. Take a deep, slow breath in, then exhale slowly. Repeat this deep breathing three times, feeling your body relax with each breath.

Envision someone who embodies pure, selfless love for you, like Jesus. Place your right hand on your heart and cover it with your left hand, pressing gently to feel a warmth emanating into your heart. Then, relax your hands into a comfortable position.

With this image in your mind, silently offer this loving person blessings for a few minutes: "May you be happy. May you be peaceful. May you be free from suffering."

Now, imagine Jesus or that person who embodies uncon-ditional love sitting beside you, offering you the same blessings. Personalize these words, repeating them to yourself for about five minutes: "May I be happy. May I be peaceful. May I be free from suffering." Feel each word as a blessing washing over you. If you wish, after a time, shorten the mantra to three words: "Happy. Peaceful. Free." Bask in the love these words bring.

Next, think of a loved one and silently offer them the same blessings for a few minutes. Then, gradually expand this circle to include friends, family, and groups you are part of, like members of your workplace or community.

Next, consider someone you might have difficulties with or haven't forgiven yet. Extend these blessings to them too: "May you be happy. May you be peaceful. May you be free from suffering."

Finally, broaden your focus to include all people in your country and, eventually, all humanity. Visualize people from diverse backgrounds—different cultures, ethnicities, religions, political beliefs, socioeconomic statuses, and lifestyles—and silently bless them.

Once your blessing feels complete, as you slowly open your eyes, conclude the meditation with heartfelt thanks: "Thank you! Thank you!"

Regular practice of this meditation can significantly enhance your sense of mental wellbeing. It's a powerful way to cultivate an expansive, loving heart that embraces all beings.

Remember that every moment and every breath offer a chance to reconnect with the infinite well of peace, love, and wisdom at the core of your being. Just as Desmond Doss repeatedly chose love over fear, you, too, can live from a higher consciousness that rises above life's challenges. The power to transform your world isn't something you must seek outside of yourself—it's already within you. And as you awaken to this deeper essence, your life, like Doss's, will quietly radiate love and peace, becoming a source of healing, wisdom, and limitless possibility in a world longing for hope.

BIBLIOGRAPHY

Anonymous. *A Course in Miracles*. Foundation for Inner Peace, 1976.

Beck, Martha. *The Way of Integrity: Finding the Path to Your True Self*. The Open Field, 2021.

Brooks, Arthur C., and Oprah Winfrey. *Build the Life You Want: The Art and Science of Getting Happier*. Portfolio, 2023.

Childre, Doc Lew, and Howard Martin. *The HeartMath Solution: The Institute of HeartMath's Revolutionary Program for Engaging the Power of the Heart's Intelligence*. HarperOne, 2000.

Cooper, David A. *God Is a Verb: Kabbalah and the Practice of Mystical Judaism*. Riverhead, 1998.

Delio, Ilia. *The Unbearable Wholeness of Being: God, Evolution, and the Power of Love*. Orbis, 2013.

Dispenza, Joe. *Breaking the Habit of Being Yourself: How to Lose Your Mind and Create a New One*. Hay House, 2012.

Douglas-Klotz, Neil. *The Hidden Gospel: Decoding the Spiritual Message of the Aramaic Jesus*. Quest Books, 2001.

———. *Original Meditation: Experiencing the Wisdom of the Aramaic Jesus*. Skylight Paths, 2011.

———. *Revelations of the Aramaic Jesus: The Hidden Teachings on Life and Living*. Hampton Roads, 2022.

Keltner, Dacher. *Awe: The New Science of Everyday Wonder and How It Can Transform Your Life*. Penguin, 2023.

Lanza, Robert. *Biocentrism: How Life and Consciousness Are the Keys to Understanding the True Nature of the Universe*. BenBella, 2009.

———. *The Grand Biocentric Design: How Life Creates Reality*. BenBella, 2020.

McLaren, Brian. *Do I Stay Christian? A Guide for the Doubters, the Disappointed, and the Disillusioned*. St. Martin's, 2022.

Päs, Heinrich. *The One: How an Ancient Idea Holds the Future of Physics*. Basic Books, 2023.

Perry, Bruce, and Oprah Winfrey. *What Happened to You? Conversations on Trauma, Resilience, and Healing*. Flatiron, 2021.

Rohr, Richard. *Immortal Diamond: The Search for Our True Self.* Jossey-Bass, 2013.

———. *The Universal Christ: How a Forgotten Reality Can Change Everything We See, Hope For, and Believe.* Convergent, 2019.

Schäfer, Lothar. *Infinite Potential: What Quantum Physics Reveals About How We Should Live.* Deepak Chopra, 2013.

Teilhard de Chardin, Pierre. *The Divine Milieu: An Essay on the Interior Life.* Harper Perennial, 2001.

———. *The Phenomenon of Man.* Harper Perennial Modern Classics, 2008.

Tolle, Eckhart. *A New Earth: Awakening to Your Life's Purpose.* Penguin, 2005.

———. *Stillness Speaks.* New World Library, 2003.

Van der Kolk, Bessel. *The Body Keeps the Score: Brain, Mind, and Body in the Healing of Trauma.* Penguin, 2014.

Van Lommel, Pim. *Consciousness Beyond Life: The Science of the Near-Death Experience.* HarperOne, 2010.

Wilber, Ken. *Integral Meditation: Mindfulness as a Way to Grow Up, Wake Up, and Show Up in Your Life.* Shambhala, 2016.

———. *No Boundary: Eastern and Western Approaches to Personal Growth.* Shambhala, 2001.

ENDNOTES

Introduction

1. American Psychological Association, *Stress in America: Paying with Our Health* (American Psychological Association, 2015), https://www. apa.org/news/press/releases/stress/2015/impact.
2. Anxiety and Depression Association of America, "Facts & Statistics," Anxiety and Depression Association of America, accessed October 17, 2024, https://adaa.org/understanding-anxiety/facts-statistics.

1. A View from Above

1. John Archibald Wheeler, *Geons, Black Holes & Quantum Forum: A Life in Physics* (W.W. Norton, 1998).
2. Robert Lanza and Bob Berman, *Biocentrism: How Life and Consciousness are the Keys to Understanding the True Nature of the Universe* (BenBella, 2010).
3. Heinrich Päs, *The One: How an Ancient Idea Holds the Future of Physics* (Basic Books, 2023).
4. Roger Penrose and Stuart Hameroff, "Consciousness in the Universe: A Review of the 'Orch OR' Theory," *Physics of Life Reviews* 11, no. 1 (2014): 39–78, https://doi.org/10.1016/j.plrev.2013. 08.002.
5. Acts 17:28. Scripture passages are my own translation.
6. Ephesians 4:6.
7. Colossians 3:11.
8. John 1:4.
9. John 17:16.
10. Matthew 22:39.
11. Neil Douglas-Klotz, Revelations of the Aramaic Jesus: The Hidden Teachings on Life and Living (Hampton Roads Publishing, 2022), p. 21.
12. John 8:32.
13. Jalal al-Din Rumi, *The Essential Rumi*, trans. Coleman Barks (HarperSanFrancisco, 1995), 106.

2. The Chaos Within the Mind

1. Ethan Kross, *Chatter: The Voice in Our Head, Why It Matters, and How to Harness It* (Crown Publishing, 2021), 35.
2. Paulina Puchalska-Wasyl, "Types of Inner Dialogues and Functions They Serve," *Journal of Constructivist Psychology* 18, no. 2 (2006): 253–275, https://doi.org/10.1080/10720530590914778.
3. Ephesians 3:19, emphasis added.

3. Reshaping Our Reality

1. Daniel J. Siegel, *The Developing Mind: How Relationships and the Brain Interact to Shape Who We Are*, 2nd ed. (Guilford Press, 2012), 312–316.

4. Know Thyself

1. Lanza and Berman, *Biocentrism*, 9.
2. Lanza and Berman, *Biocentrism*, 16.
3. John 1:1.

5. The Vibrational Signature

1. Rollin McCraty, *The Energetic Heart: Bioelectromagnetic Interactions Within and Between People* (Institute of HeartMath, 2003), 10.
2. Neil Douglas-Klotz, *Revelations of the Aramaic Jesus: The Hidden Teachings on Life and Living* (Hampton Roads, 2022), 35.
3. Douglas-Klotz, *Revelations of the Aramaic Jesus*, 35.
4. Matthew 6:33.
5. Luke 17:21.
6. Matthew 19:26.
7. John 3:1–21.
8. Neil Douglas-Klotz, *Original Meditation: Experiencing the Wisdom of the Aramaic Jesus* (Skylight Paths, 2011), 124.
9. Matthew 3:2.

6. The Barrier of the Ego

1. Rumi, *Essential Rumi*, 199. For additional context, see Rumi, *The Book of Love: Poems of Ecstasy and Longing*, trans. Coleman Barks (HarperOne, 2005).
2. In Eckhart Tolle's book *A New Earth: Awakening to Your Life's Purpose*, the concept of the ego is dissected into two primary components: content and structure. Tolle explains that understanding the ego can initially seem complex, but it becomes more manageable when these two elements are considered. Content refers to the specific thoughts, beliefs, and identifications that make up the ego, while structure pertains to the underlying patterns and mechanisms through which the ego operates.
3. Galatians 2:20.
4. Psalm 46:10.
5. Colossians 1:27.

7. Light on Shadows

1. Joe Dispenza, *Breaking the Habit of Being Yourself: How to Lose Your Mind and Create a New One* (Hay House, 2012), 79–81.
2. Daniel J. Siegel, *The Developing Mind: How Relationships and the Brain Interact to Shape Who We Are* (Guilford Press, 2012) discusses how early experiences shape our personality and sense of self. See also Robert McCrae and Paul Costa, *Personality in Adulthood: A Five-Factor Theory Perspective* (Guilford Press, 2003), which explores the stability of personality traits throughout adulthood. Additionally, Carol Dweck's *Mindset: The New Psychology of Success* (Random House, 2006) addresses how beliefs and perceptions formed early in life influence behavior and self-concept.
3. Bessel van der Kolk, *The Body Keeps the Score: Brain, Mind, and Body in the Healing of Trauma* (Penguin, 2014), 70–72.
4. John 8:32.
5. Jeremiah 17:9. For further discussion on the interpretation of this verse, see *The Expositor's Bible Commentary*, ed. Frank E. Gaebelein (Zondervan, 1984), 580. Additionally, *Jeremiah: A Commentary* by J. A. Thompson (Westminster John Knox Press, 1980) provides insights into the cultural and theological implications of Jeremiah's writings.
6. McCraty, *The Energetic Heart*, 8. For additional insights, see Doc Childre and Howard Martin, *The HeartMath Solution: The Institute of*

HeartMath's Revolutionary Program for Engaging the Power of the Heart's Intelligence (HarperOne, 1999), 26.

7. McCraty, *The Energetic Heart*, 12. For further details, see Childre and Martin, *The HeartMath Solution*, 40.
8. Douglas-Klotz, *Revelations of the Aramaic Jesus*, 1.
9. Psalm 4:4.
10. Ephesians 1:18.
11. McCraty, *The Energetic Heart*, 14. See also Herbert Benson, *The Relaxation Response* (HarperTorch, 2000), 90–92, which discusses the physiological benefits of meditation. Additionally, Richard J. Davidson and Bruce S. McEwen, "Social Influences on Neuroplasticity: Stress and Interventions to Promote Well-Being," *Nature Neuroscience*, 2012, explores the impact of meditation on stress hormone production and cardiovascular health.
12. Sara W. Lazar et al., "Meditation Experience is Associated with Increased Cortical Thickness," *NeuroReport*, 2005, 16(17): 1893–1897. See also Richard J. Davidson et al., "Alterations in Brain and Immune Function Produced by Mindfulness Meditation," *Psychosomatic Medicine*, 2003, 65(4): 564–570. For further reading, see Norman A. S. Farb et al., "Minding One's Emotions: Mindfulness Training Alters the Neural Expression of Sadness," *Emotion*, 2010, 10(1): 25–33. Additionally, see Benson, *The Relaxation Response*, 112–114, for discussions on meditation and its impact on the brain and immune system.

8. Navigating Our Inner Maps

1. Jean Piaget, *The Origins of Intelligence in Children* (International Universities Press, 1952) discusses Piaget's theory of cognitive development stages. See Ken Wilber, *Integral Psychology: Consciousness, Spirit, Psychology, Therapy* (Shambhala, 2000) for an exploration of Wilber's integral theory and stages of consciousness. Additionally, James Fowler, *Stages of Faith: The Psychology of Human Development and the Quest for Meaning* (HarperOne, 1981) elaborates on Fowler's stages of faith development. For further context, see *The Collected Works of Ken Wilber, Volume 2: The Atman Project; Up from Eden* (Shambhala, 1999), which provides comprehensive insights into Wilber's developmental models.
2. Ken Wilber, *The Spectrum of Consciousness*, 2nd ed. (Quest, 1993), 120.
3. Wilber, *Integral Psychology*, 67.

4. Ken Wilber, *A Brief History of Everything*, 2nd ed. (Shambhala, 2007), 215.

5. Ken Wilber, *The Integral Vision: A Very Short Introduction to the Revolutionary Integral Approach to Life, God, the Universe, and Everything* (Shambhala, 2007), 89.

6. Ken Wilber, *A Theory of Everything: An Integral Vision for Business, Politics, Science, and Spirituality* (Shambhala, 2001), 120.

7. Pierre Teilhard de Chardin, *The Divine Milieu* (Harper & Row, 1960), 92. For additional context, see *Teilhard de Chardin: Writings Selected with an Introduction by Ursula King* (Orbis, 1999), which provides insights into Teilhard's thoughts on the intersection of science, faith, and consciousness.

8. Luke 23:34.

9. The Heart as a Conduit

1. Joseph E. LeDoux, *The Emotional Brain: The Mysterious Underpinnings of Emotional Life* (Simon & Schuster, 1996), 158–162. See also Eric R. Kandel, James H. Schwartz, and Thomas M. Jessell, *Principles of Neural Science* (McGraw-Hill, 2000), 983–986, for detailed insights into the functions of the amygdala. Additionally, consult John P. Aggleton, *The Amygdala: A Functional Analysis* (Oxford University Press, 2000) for comprehensive coverage of the amygdala's role in emotional processing and response.

2. "Translation of the Shema," *Chabad*, https://www.chabad.org/library/article_cdo/aid/706162/jewish/Translation.htm.

10. The Melody Within

1. John 14:27.
2. John 20:21–22.
3. Hebrews 12:2.

11. The Wisdom Within

1. Gershom Scholem, *Kabbalah* (Dorset Press, 1987), 215–218.

12. A Life of Awe

1. Julian of Norwich, *Revelations of Divine Love*, trans. Elizabeth Spearing (Penguin, 1998), 135. For additional context, see *Julian of Norwich: Showings*, ed. Edmund Colledge and James Walsh (Paulist, 1978), which provides a comprehensive exploration of her mystical experiences and theological insights.
2. Chris Hadfield, *An Astronaut's Guide to Life on Earth* (Little, Brown, 2013), 45. For additional insights, see his 2014 TED Talk, "What I Learned from Going Blind in Space," https://www.ted.com/talks/ chris_hadfield_what_i_learned_from_going_blind_in_space.
3. Nicole Stott, as quoted in "Space for Humanity: The Impact of Seeing Earth from Space," *National Geographic*, 2019, 112. Further details can be found in her interviews and NASA's reports on astronaut experiences.
4. Albert Einstein, as quoted in *The World as I See It* (Philosophical Library, 1949), 5. Additional context is available in Walter Isaacson, *Einstein: His Life and Universe* (Simon & Schuster, 2007), which explores his philosophical and scientific contributions.

ABOUT THE AUTHOR

David Youngren, a Swedish-born spiritual philosopher, storyteller, and philanthropist, has spoken to over one million people at live events. As founder of Limitless Research International, he explores fundamental questions of existence, God, and consciousness, aiming to inspire lasting transformation and nurture mental and spiritual wellbeing.

Earlier in his life, Youngren led large-scale evangelistic campaigns, founded a Bible seminary in Canada, and served as a pastor, before a profound meditation experience in 2006 shifted his focus toward inner transformation and spiritual awakening.

This new direction inspired him to create meditation programs like *The Amazing Life*, produce films such as *The Story* and *Africa Sing Me Your Song*, and write several books including *Awakening To I Am Love*. His latest book, *Life Ascending* integrates timeless wisdom and modern science to offer a transformative guide to mental wellbeing.

David is also the founder of Juma's World, a charity empowering orphaned children in Tanzania. He now lives in San Diego, California, with his wife, Kim, and they enjoy spending time with their two adult children and their families.